A Prov

by

Peter Gill

from a story by Anton Chekhov

Performed 1–17 March 2012
Sherman Cymru, Cardiff

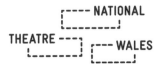

CAST

Kezia Burrows
Alex Clatworthy
Richard Corgan
Helen Griffin
Lee Haven-Jones
Mike Hayward
Mark Lewis
Sara Lloyd-Gregory
John-Paul Macleod
Liam Mansfield
Clive Merrison
Kenneth Price
Nicholas Shaw
William Thomas
Menna Trussler

CREATIVE TEAM

Directed by **Peter Gill**
Designed by **Alison Chitty**
Lighting Design by **Paul Pyant**
Composed by **Terry Davies**
Sound Designer **Mike Beer**
for Stage Sound Services

Assistant Director **Julia Thomas**
(part of National Theatre Wales' Emerging Director Scheme)
Assistant Designer **Louie Whitemore**
Props Supervisor **Jane Slattery**
Costume Supervisor **Carrie Bayliss**
Wigs Supervisor **Joyce Beagarie**
Production Manager **David Evans**
Company Stage Manager **Matthew North**
Deputy Stage Manager **Rachel Burgess**
Assistant Stage Manager **Ryan Tate**
Head of Wardrobe **Jo Reynolds**
Observer Assistant Designer **Kitty Callister**
Observer Assistant Designer **Holly Pigott**
Student Stage Manager **Rhodri Hunt**
Promoter **Anna Poole**

Ensemble

John Atkinson, Luke Bridgeman, Abigail Fitzgerald, Heledd Gwynn,
Kristian Jenkins, Jan Jones, Ryan Nolan, Clare Parry Jones, Ian Phillips,
John Redpath, Liane Walters, John Williams

NATIONAL

THEATRE

WALES

National Theatre Wales was launched in November 2009, and creates invigorating theatre in the English language, rooted in Wales, with an international reach. To date, it has staged 16 productions in locations all over Wales, at the Edinburgh Festival Fringe and the London International Mime Festival. In October 2011, National Theatre Wales was described as 'one of the best things to happen to the stage in the past five years' by *The Observer.*

For more information, visit: nationaltheatrewales.org

Past productions include: *A Good Night Out in the Valleys*; *The Devil Inside Him*; *The Persians* (winner of the Ted Hughes Award for Poetry and TMA Award for Best Design); *The Passion* – 'one of the outstanding theatrical events not only of this year, but of the decade' (*The Observer*) – and *The Village Social.*

National Theatre Wales is supported by Arts Council of Wales and the Welsh Government.

National Theatre Wales
30 Castle Arcade
Cardiff / CF10 1BW

Phone +44 (0)29 2035 3070
info@nationaltheatrewales.org
nationaltheatrewales.org

Twitter: @ntwtweets

To keep up to date with the latest information, text NTW Y2 to 61211.

Cyngor Celfyddydau Cymru
Arts Council of Wales

Noddir gan
Lywodraeth Cymru
Sponsored by
Welsh Government

NATIONAL THEATRE WALES

Cast

Kezia Burrows Anyuta Ivanova Blagovo

Trained at RADA. Theatre includes: *Venice Preserved* (Arcola), *A Man for All Seasons, Kind Hearts and Coronets, To Kill a Mockingbird* (PFT), *The Merchant of Venice* (Creation), *The Misanthrope, The Bald Prima Donna* (London Rd), *Much Ado About Nothing* (YSC), *Measure for Measure* (Sherman). TV includes: *CRASH* (BBC), *Casualty* (BBC), *Phoneshop* (E4). Film includes: *Capgras Tide* (Upstart), *The Way of the Monkey's Claw* (Nowhere Fast), *With These Hands* (Room 16). Radio includes: *The Anarchist in the Basement* (Radio 4).

Alex Clatworthy Maria Victorovna Dolzhikova

Trained at the Guildhall School of Music and Drama, where she won the 2011 Michael Bryant Award. Theatre credits include: *Sleeping Beauty* (Birmingham Rep) and *Big Brother is Watching You* (Sherman Cymru). Television credits include: *Henry IV Parts One & Two* directed by Sir Richard Eyre (BBC), *Axon, The Bench* and *Want 2TLK Science?* (BBC Wales), *Treflan* (Alfresco), *Pawb At Y Bwrdd* and *Hotel Eddie* (Apollo). Radio credits include: *Evacuees* and *Meddwl* (BBC Wales).

Richard Corgan Prokofy

Trained at Bristol Old Vic Theatre School. Theatre credits include: *Flowers from Tunisia* (Torch), *Taming of the Shrew* (Globe), *Frozen* (Sherman), *It's About Me* (Hampstead), *Money, Science, Me* (Everyman), *Romeo and Juliet* (Lord Chamberlain's Men), *Ballad of Blood and Darling* (Rose Theatre), *The Long, the Short and the Tall* (Pleasance), *La Fanciulla del West* (Royal Opera House), *Macbeth, The Changeling* (Barbican), *Phoenix and The Carpet* (Bristol Old Vic) Television includes: *Baker Boys, Doctors, Casualty, Caught in the Web, The B Word* (BBC). Film includes: *Magpie, Colin, Hindsight*. Radio includes: *Blue Remembered Hills*

Helen Griffin Madame Azhogina

Theatre credits include: *The Devil Inside Him* (National Theatre Wales) *Small Change, Shadow of a Boy*, the acclaimed one-woman show *Caitlin* (Sherman Cymru); *Cymbeline* (Ludlow Festival). TV includes: *Coronation Street; Getting On; Criminal Justice Two; Vivian Vyle Show; Con Passionata; Dr Who: The Age Of Steel; Casualty; The Bill*. Film includes: *Little White Lies* (Bafta Cymru Best Actress 2007), *Risen, Human Traffic*. Her one-woman show *Who's Afraid of Rachel Roberts* tours Wales in May (Torch Theatre).

Lee Haven-Jones Boris Ivanov Blagovo

is a Clwyd Theatre Cymru Associate. Theatre credits include: *Mary Stuart, Festen* and *Arcadia* (Theatr Clwyd), *Memory* and *Night Must Fall* (Theatr Clwyd/59E59 Theatre, NYC), *The Pull of Negative Gravity* (Traverse Theatre), *Romeo and Juliet* (Theatr Genedlaethol Cymru), and *The Bacchai* (National Theatre). Television credits include: *Gwaith Cartref* (Fiction Factory), *Caerdydd* (S4C) and *Love in a Cold Climate* (BBC). Film credits include *The Prince* and *Perfect Day*. Television directing credits include: *Indian Doctor* (BBC) and *Alys* (S4C).

Mike Hayward Shopkeeper / Berlichev

For the National Theatre: *Anthony and Cleopatra, Animal Farm* (tour Europe, Canada and America), *The Party, Marriage of Figaro* (directors: Jonathan Miller, Peter Hall, David Hare); St George's Theatre: title role in *Macbeth. Under Milk Wood*, director Sir Anthony Hopkins; one-man show: A L Kennedy's *Just About Ready* (Edinburgh Fringe First, British Council Tour, India and Sri Lanka. TV includes six years in *Take the High Road*, as Alun Morgan), *Little Britain*.

Mark Lewis Victor Ivanov Dolzhikov

Trained at the Central School of Speech and Drama and for many years was associated with the Citizens Theatre, Glasgow. He has worked at the National Theatre, The Royal Exchange, The Riverside, The Donmar, The Arcola, among others and worked with writer/directors such as Howard Barker and Steven Berkoff. He has appeared in TV series, films and radio.

Sara Lloyd-Gregory
Cleopatra Alexandrovna Polozneva

Trained at the Royal Welsh College of Music and Drama. Theatre credits include: *Up 'n' Under* (Black Rat), *Romeo and Juliet* (Wales Theatre Co), *The American Pilot* and *A Midsummer Night's Dream* (RWCMD). Television credits include: *Alys, Con Passionate, Y Pris* (S4C), *Thorne: Sleepyhead* (Sky 1), *Tess of the D'Urbervilles, Torchwood, Belonging* (BBC), *Sleep With Me* and *Affinity* (ITV). Film credits include: *Little White Lies* (Red & Black Films), *A Way of Life* (AWOL Films). Radio credits include: *Last Tango in Aberystwyth* (BBC Radio 4).

John-Paul MacLeod   Ivan Mikhailovich Cheprakov

Trained at RADA. Theatre includes: *Spies* (Theatre Alibi), *King Lear* (Headlong/ Liverpool Everyman) directed by Rupert Goold, *Passion* (NTW) directed by Michael Sheen, *All Night I Dream about Being Good* (The Yard Hackney). Television includes: *Casualty* (BBC), *Doctors* (BBC), My *Boy Jack* (ITV). Film: *Small Miracles* (Snake River), *To Kill a King* (Fairfax Films), *Calendar Girls* (Buena Vista)

Liam Mansfield   Workman / Guest

Trained at Mountview Academy of Theatre Arts and graduated in June 2011. Theatre credits include: *Under Milk Wood* (Farnham Rep), *Fameless* (Sotto Voce), *24 Hour Plays: Old Vic New Voices* (Old Vic Theatre), *A Christmas Carol* (Maxim Theatre, Stockholm). Film credits include: *Ushers* (Jukka Productions)

Clive Merrison   Alexandr Pavlovich Poloznev

Recent theatre: *The History Boys* (NT and Broadway), *Credible Witness* (Royal Court), *The Cocktail Party* (Lyceum), *The Madness of George III* (NT and Broadway). Recent TV: *Peep Show*, *Monday Monday*, *Egypt*, *Foyle's War*, *Julius Caesar*. Clive will appear in *Bert and Dickie* for the BBC in 2012. Film includes: *History Boys*, *Saving Grace*, *The English Patient* and *Heavenly Creatures.*

Kenneth Price   Governor of the Province / Old Man

Trained at the Bristol Old Vic Theatre School and his extensive theatre work includes seasons at Scarborough, Manchester Royal Exchange, Bristol Old Vic, Keswick, Salisbury and the West End. His film credits include, *John and Yoko, Fierce Creatures* and *Diana and Me,* while his numerous television appearances include *Emmerdale, The Atomic Inferno, Casualty, The Chief, A Touch of Spice* and *The Bill.*

Nicholas Shaw Misail Alexandrovich Poloznev
Training: Drama Centre London. Theatre credits include:
Phaedra's Love (Arcola, London), *Hamlet* (Northern
Broadsides), *'Tis Pity She's a Whore* and *Anthology*
(Liverpool Everyman/Slung Low), *The Fairy Queen*
(Glyndebourne/Opera Comique/BAM), *Romeo and Juliet*
and *A Midsummer Night's Dream* (Open Air Theatre,
Regent's Park), *Merchant of Venice* and *Holding Fire!*
(Shakespeare's Globe), *Easter* (Oxford Stage Company),
for which he received an Ian Charleson Award commen-
dation. Television credits include; *Land Girls, The
Rotters' Club, The Romantics* (BBC); *Foyle's War,
Afterlife* (ITV); *Goldplated* (Channel 4).

William Thomas Andrey Ivanov

William's work spans four decades, and he received a
nomination for Best Actor at the BAFTA Cymru Awards
(2007) for his portrayal of Glyn in the award winning
Con Passionate. Other television credits include *Doctor
Who, Midsomer Murders, Alys, Gavin and Stacey,
Belonging* (10 Series), *Grass, Fun at the Funeral Parlour*
and *We Are Seven.* William also plays Geraint Cooper in
the BBC and US series *Torchwood.* Film credits includes
Mr Nice (Kodak Award Winner); *Assassin in Love*
(RiverRun International Film Festival Winner); *Longitude*
(2001 BAFTA Winner for Best Drama Serial); Oscar
nominated & BAFTA Award winning *Solomon and
Gaenor;* and *Twin Town.*

Menna Trussler Karpovna / Madame Mufke

Theatre credits include: *Swansea Girls, Gypsy, Cabaret,
Side by Side by Sondheim, Puss in Boots, 84 Charing
Cross Road, Midsummer Night's Dream* and *Cinderella*
(Swansea Grand), *Bedside Manners, The Drag Factor,
Green Favours, Roots and Wings, Sleeping with Mickey
Mouse, Loose Ends* and *A Kiss on the Bottom* (Sherman
Theatre), *Tartuffe* (Clwyd Theatr Cymru), *Family
Planning* (Grass Roots). Television credits include: *Stella*
(Sky), *Come Fly With Me, Crash, Jam and Jerusalem*
(3 series), *Torchwood II, Casualty, Doctors, Little Britain*
(3 series), *The Bench, Hope and Glory, Trip Trap, Rainbow Chaser, Boy Soldier*
and *Thicker Than Water* (BBC); *Alys, Y Pris, Os Byw Ac Iach, Bydd Yn Wrol,
Pam Fi Duw?, Pobol Y Cwm* (S4C); *In the Company of Strangers, Ballroom,
Better Days* and *We Are Seven* (HTV); *Liquorice Alsorts* (Daffodil Productions).
Film credits include: *There She Goes* (Short Films), *Rhestr Nadolig Wil* (Boom
Film), *Caught in the Act* (Carnaby Films), *Family Ties* (Beryl Productions),
Plotz with a View (CFI Films), *Human Traffic* (Fruit Salad Films), *August*
(Granada Films). Radio credits include: *Writing the Century 14, A Burden to
Strangers – The Diaries of Rachel Minshall* (BBC Radio 4), *Ceri Elen* (BBC
Radio Cymru).

Creative Team

Peter Gill   Director

Peter was born in 1939 in Cardiff and started his professional career as an actor. A director as well as a writer, he has directed over 100 productions in the UK, Europe and North America in both the modern and classical repertoires, including plays by Chekhov, Congreve, Otway, Shakespeare, as well as Hampton, Orton, Osborne, Pinter and Wright. At the Royal Court Theatre in the 1960s he was responsible for introducing D.H. Lawrence's plays to the theatre and was the founding director of Riverside Studios and the Royal National Theatre Studio. Classical plays directed include: *The Importance of Being Earnest* by Oscar Wilde (Theatre Royal Bath, Tour & Vaudeville Theatre, 2008); Gaslight (Old Vic, 2007), *Look Back in Anger* (Theatre Royal Bath, 2006), *The Voysey Inheritance* (NT, 2006), and *Romeo and Juliet* (RSC, 2004-5). Other directed work includes: *The Breath of Life* by David Hare (Sheffield Theatres, 2011); *The Aliens* by Annie Baker (Bush Theatre, 2010); *Semper Dowland* and *The Corridor* by Harrison Birtwistle (Aldeburgh Festival / Southbank Centre, 2009); *Epitaph for George Dillon* by John Osborne and Anthony Creighton (ATG, 2005); *Days of Wine and Roses* by J.P. Miller, in a new version by Owen McCafferty (Donmar Warehouse, 2005); *Scenes from the Big Picture* by Owen McCafferty (NT, 2003); and *Speed the Plough* by David Mamet (ATG, 2000).

Peter's plays include: *Another Door Closed* (Theatre Royal Bath, 2009); *Small Change* (Donmar Warehouse, 2008); *The York Realist* (English Touring Theatre at the Royal Court, 2002); *Original Sin* (Crucible Sheffield, 2002); *The Look Across the Eyes* and *Lovely Evening* (BBC Radio 4, 2001); *Certain Young Men* (Almeida, 1999); *Friendly Fire* (NT, 1998–9); *Cardiff East* (NT, 1995); *Mean Tears* (NT, 1987); *In the Blue* (NT, 1985); *Small Change* (NT, 1983); *Kick for Touch* (NT, 1983); *The Sleepers Den* (Royal Court, 1969) and *Over Gardens Out* (Royal Court, 1969).

Alison Chitty   Designer

Alison has a distinguished international career in theatre, opera and film. Her theatre credits include eight years as resident designer at the National Theatre where she designed many productions, including *Venice Preserv'd*, *Antony and Cleopatra*, *The Bacchae*, *The Voysey Inheritance* and Mike Leigh's *Two Thousand Years*. She has just designed Mike Leigh's new play *Grief*. She has designed in opera houses throughout the world, including Chicago, Seattle, Munich and Paris. Recently she designed the highly acclaimed world premiere of Harrison Birtwistle's *The Minotaur* at the Royal Opera House Covent Garden, and *Rigoletto* for La Fenice, Venice. Her film credits include: *Aria*, *Turn of the Screw*, and several Mike Leigh films including *Life is Sweet*, *Naked* and *Secrets and Lies*.

In recognition of her particular approach to teaching and her commitment to developing the talent of young theatre designers and practitioners, Alison was awarded the Misha Black Award in 2006, The Young Vic Award in 2008 and a Fellowship at Birkbeck, London University, in 2011.

Terry Davies Composer

Terry has written for many theatre productions at the National Theatre, RSC, West End, around the UK and elsewhere. His productions with Peter Gill include *The Aliens* (Bush), *Look Back in Anger* (Theatre Royal, Bath), *The Voysey Inheritance* (NT), *Romeo and Juliet* (RSC), *Original Sin* (Sheffield) and *The York Realist* (English Touring Theatre/Royal Court). He is an artistic associate of choreographer Matthew Bourne, composing for his *Lord of the Flies, Dorian Gray, Edward Scissorhands, The Car Man* and *Play Without Words*, for which he received an Olivier Award. He has conducted the music for nearly 50 films including *W.E., The King's Speech, The Illusionist, Another Year* and *Brideshead Revisited*.

Paul Pyant Lighting Designer

Paul is a graduate of the Royal Academy of Dramatic Art, and works in opera, ballet, musicals and theatre worldwide. He has a long-established association with Glyndebourne Opera, English National Opera, The Royal Opera, Covent Garden, National Theatre, English National Ballet, The Donmar Warehouse, The Almeida Theatre and Northern Ballet Theatre. Recent productions include: *Grief* (National Theatre), *Richard III* (Old Vic), *Aspects of Love* (Menier Chocolate Factory), *House of Games* (Almeida), *Betrothal in a Monastery* (Théâtre du Capitole and Opera Comique), *The Heretic* (Royal Court), and *Hobson's Choice* (Crucible Theatre, Sheffield).

Peter Gill
A Provincial Life

from a story by
ANTON CHEKHOV

faber and faber

First published in 2012
by Faber and Faber Ltd
74–77 Great Russell Street
London WC1B 3DA

Typeset by Country Setting, Kingsdown, Kent CT14 8ES
Printed in England by CPI Group (UK) Ltd, Croydon CR0 4YY

A CIP record for this book
is available from the British Library

978-0-571-29040-6

FSC
www.fsc.org
MIX
Paper from
responsible sources
FSC® C101712

2 4 6 8 10 9 7 5 3 1

To Susan Engel

Foreword

There can be few bodies of work that are as rewarding when read continuously as the plays of Peter Gill. From the beginning of his career, his theatre has been engaged in a Van Gogh-like search, not quite to find the beauty in a pair of old boots, but rather to reveal a beauty that is always present in anything, weathered or leather or otherwise. This hard stare at the ordinary world, his extraordinary way of seeing, connects each new play to the last like beads on a rosary. To read Gill's plays chronologically is to witness the expansion and unfolding of both a mind and a world, beautiful and distinctive, made richer and more compelling with each new statement.

A Provincial Life was an early statement. Written in 1966 because Gill was, as he puts it, 'incredibly touched' by Chekhov's story, it was presented on the set of another Royal Court production for one night. The play came very early in Gill's career. At the time of writing he was moving in precisely the opposite direction to his hero, Misail, who quits bourgeois society for the 'real life' of the country – Gill, who had moved from Cardiff to London, denies realising that opposition as he wrote, but the coincidence is interesting. Throughout Gill's work, influence and motivation are revealing: the Beckettian idea of 'no symbols where none intended' applies, as references bubble up from the subconscious into the dialogue without being planned. He is aware Proust is quoted in *Small Change*, but denies knowing at the time of writing that the titles of two of his plays – *Small Change* and *The Sleepers Den* – are drawn from the poetry of Donne. This is part of what makes Gill so rewarding to read – he is an instinctive writer, and influences in his work are the organisations of the preconscious mind, collecting the nebulous material of a subconscious into a statement.

Patterned throughout *A Provincial Life* are moving examples of Gill's eye for the minutiae of human life – for care, worry, and love. People reach out to one another throughout Gill's work, and it is no different here – when Misail's father asks him, 'Are you all right? You're looking pale. Have you been feeling unwell again?', a distance between two people is revealed, and their attempts to cross it, to care for one another, are shown to be snagged in the inadequate medium of speech. Misail says later in the play to his father, 'I love you. I am unutterably sorry that we are apart.' That 'unutterably' is at the centre of the play. Characters attempt to put words to the feeling time and again, however, because 'one must love. We ought to love oughtn't we?' This impulse, the need to love, is the motivating power behind Gill's work, and the materials of his theatre, the elements which complicate and humanise love, are the particularities of everyday life – Gill expresses the emotional trajectory of so much of his writing when he has Misail say, 'Sometimes I think such marvellous things and dream such brilliant conclusions but my thoughts are always broken by visions of rissoles or bowls of porridge.' The movement from the idea to the specific that contains but also expresses the emotion recurs in play after play.

What we watch in *A Provincial Life* is a struggle to come to terms with life: an attempt to find meaning in it, to accommodate frustration and bear the fact that life is passing you by each second you are living it. Misail tries to drown his anxieties in work, but the attempt is a vain one. It is among the details of the world, the rissoles and bowls of porridge, that meaning is lost. This 'drowning' in life is inevitable. Like any emotion, a life is always caged into the specifics of a body, a home town, a world – but in Gill's work the way that happens, and the way the emotion and life show through, become the focus of attention, making beautiful a struggle that might at first appear as empty of love as a pair of old boots.

This is perhaps the reason Gill has been drawn to Chekhov, as he has been throughout his career. The constant ebb of life, as it flows past and away from his characters, is distinctive in Gill's treatments and translations. Engaging with Chekhov allows Gill to come to express the idea that life and love are elsewhere, lost in simile, only recognised afterwards, seen across a distance. What meaning there is in Misail's life becomes all of these when he says, 'She is like a green parrot that had escaped and used to fly in the gardens of a square where I used to work.' Life and love seem very far away from Cleopatra when she asks, 'What is it that stops people from acting as they really desire?', not knowing that the person she is speaking to has fallen asleep. Gill asks this question in all his work – in *Small Change*, Gerard asks, 'What is it, what is it that will find the moment, that will . . .' That moment, that meaning, is elusive – but Gill reminds us that it is out there, hidden in the details of living.

Barney Norris
February 2012

Acknowledgements

Peter Gill would like to record with gratitude
the members of the cast of the original production
of this play at the Royal Court Theatre, London,
on 30 October 1966

Jean Boht
Pamela Buchner
Richard Butler
George Canell
Oliver Cotton
Anne Dyson
Susan Engel
Bernard Gallagher
Amaryllis Garnet
Jean Holness
Anthony Hopkins
William Hoyland
Peter John
Gillian Martell
Rosemary McHale
John McKelvey
John Normington
Richard O'Callaghan
Shivaun O'Casey
Trevor Peacock
Toby Salaman
Charlotte Selwyn
John Shepherd
Geoffrey Whitehead
Peter Wyatt

Characters

Misail Alexandrovich Poloznev

Alexandr Pavlovich Poloznev
his father, an architect

Cleopatra Alexandrovna Polozneva
his sister

Anyuta Ivanovna Blagovo
their friend

Ivan Mikhailovich Cheprakov
a school friend of Misail

Andrey Ivanov
a working man and contractor

Boris Ivanovich Blagovo
Anyuta's brother, a doctor in the army

Viktor Ivanovich Dolzhikov
an engineer

A Shopkeeper

A Workman

Other Workmen

Maria Viktorovna Dolzhikova
Dolzhikov's daughter

An Old Man

Karpovna
Misail and Cleopatra's old nurse

Prokofy
her son, a butcher

Madame Azhogina

Madame Mufke
an amateur actress

Berlichev
a guest at Madame Azhogina's

The Governor of the Province

Madame Azhogina's Daughters

Guests

Place: a Russian province in the 1890s

A PROVINCIAL LIFE

Alexandr Pavlovitch Poloznev's house. Misail Alexandr is reading a play. Cleopatra Alexandrovna enters with a tray.

Cleopatra I've brought you something to eat. (*Pause.*) Father knows you're back. He's in the study. (*She coughs.*) Misail Alexandr, why do you do this to us? You've lost your job again. I can tell. It's too bad of you.

Misail What's this?

Cleopatra Some cold meat. Did you get any dinner?

Misail No.

Cleopatra There isn't much there, I'm afraid. But Father said . . .

Misail Don't cry.

Cleopatra Think of us. Spare us. Please. You've put Father in an awful state and I'm not well. What will happen to you? Please, Misail, please don't make things worse than they are. Please. In the name of our mama, I beg you.

Misail We should not live in the present what belongs in the past.

Father (*off*) Cleopatra.

Cleopatra Papa?

Father (*enters*) Will you get my hat and stick for me, Cleopatra? Then we can go out for a walk.

Cleopatra I can't.

Father You can't?

Cleopatra Anyuta Ivanovna said she was going to call, but if you like I can send a note. (*She begins to cough.*)

Father You mustn't offend your friends. Her father is a president in court. We mustn't be rude. Are you all right? You're looking pale. Have you been feeling unwell again?

Cleopatra No. No. Shall I get your hat?

Father If you please.

She exits.

Father What is this?

Misail Cleo brought it in for me. It's some cold meat.

Father Don't let it go to waste. Well, where have you been?

Misail At work. Where else would I be?

Father You were not at work. Why do you lie? At least, you were not there this afternoon. I have here a letter from His Excellency your superintendent. I read. 'I have only kept him on out of regard for your worthy self. However, in reply to my saying that but for you he would have been free to go long before this, he replied . . .' What did you reply?

Misail I said . . .

Father What did you say?

Misail I said, 'You flatter me too much, Your Excellency, if you imagine that I am at liberty to do anything at all without my father's consent.'

Pause.

Father I see now that the hand of providence was in your mother's death, for let me tell you your behaviour would have made a longer life continually painful. You are not a child. You are gone twenty-five. You are beginning to go grey. And yet you will persist in acting like a schoolboy. At your age you should be holding down a good job like the other young men of your position in the town, but you continue to be an embarrassment, affecting the manners of people who not many years ago were serfs.

Misail Father, when I was younger and you didn't know what to do with me I went first of all into the army and then into pharmacy and then one by one took advantage of everything that was available to me as your son. You must see that I am unsuited to our kind of life.

Father And what does that mean, I should like to know. That I am to finance you while you continue along the road to God knows where, full of your own importance? That I am to approve of your friends? That I should encourage you to frequent all the low places in town at my expense? You aspire to the literary society, an organisation whose only aim, it seems to me, is to seduce the young people of the town from their religion and their duty. And all I find you do there is help paint the scenery for Madame Azhogina's amateur theatricals. Well, tomorrow we will go together and you will apologise to the superintendent and promise to work better in the future. You will take up a proper place in society with no further delay.

Misail Papa, Papa. Please. Understand. Can't you see that what you think of as a proper place in society is only the privilege of money and education? The poor and uneducated have to earn their bread by working hard for it and I don't see what rights and qualifications I have which should make me an exception to them.

Father We will not discuss your ideas of what constitutes social progress. Must I explain to you again, you brainless young idiot, that in spite of your inadequacies and apart from your physical strength you have been privileged with the divine spark – a sacred fire which distinguishes you from the beasts of the fields and the fowls of the air in the sight of God? A holy fire kindled in the best of mankind. We are a family. Your great-grandfather who fought at Borodino, your grandfather the poet and orator and Marshal of the Nobility, your uncle the educationalist and myself the municipal architect, have we, have all the Poloznevs, kept the sacred flame alight only for you, you to put it out?

Misail Father, be fair. Millions of people have to work with their hands.

Father Let them. They are fit for no better. Anyone can work with his hands. It is the sign of the barbarian. The sacred flame marks only the few.

Misail And when I sit in that office trying to compete with that typewriting machine. What has the sacred flame to do with that?

Father It is not what I had hoped for, but it seems it has to be enough. Now I warn you, Misail, if you do not go back to work directly and you go on behaving as you have been behaving, you may take it that there will be no room for you under my roof and that I shall have no more to do with you. Nor will your sister, I promise you. And perhaps what will seem more important to you, I shall take steps to see that you get nothing when I die.

Misail Papa, what I have been saying means, don't you see, that I could never accept an inheritance anyway and that whatever you decide to leave me I shall have to renounce before you die.

Father How dare you.

He strikes him.

How dare you throw all that we have to offer in our faces. You forget yourself. What are you? Who are you? You waster, you blackguard, you fool, you idiot.

Cleopatra comes in with a hat and stick.

Thank you. Give me some of God's air to clear away that fellow's nonsense. I shall only be gone a little while.

He exits. Pause.
Misail hears piano music through the window.

Misail Where's that coming from?

Cleopatra Across the street. From the engineer's house. Dolzhikov's daughter is home from St Petersburg, I believe.

Misail (*mouth full*) Oh, this spring. How it bursts each year and how new and extraordinary it always seems. It rained this afternoon.

Cleopatra I know.

Misail That was good. The trees are better for it. Look at the light shifting through the leaves. Listen to the insects. Everyone is out for his walk. Father is just bowing to Anyuta Blagovo.

Cleopatra Anyuta. She is coming to see me. And you.

Misail He is just raising his hat. It looks like one of those black chimneys he patented that he can't find a market for. Poor Father, how unimaginative he is.

Cleopatra You will not speak like that. He is our father. He is a good man. He's a good architect. Everyone respects him.

Misail I know. But you must see that he has no imagination. His houses are respected, yes, but they are all like this one. Lots of poky rooms tacked on to a huge hall, by too many doors. His work is muddled and limited. His buildings have hard, stubborn expressions. But for all that, they're timid with their low roofs. They are all alike and they're all like him. His style has become the style of this town because people have got used to his lack of any vision. His style has taken root in our lives.

The front doorbell rings.

Cleopatra That will be Anyuta Ivanovna. We have something to say to you.

She exits – he looks at the prompt script. Anyuta and Cleopatra enter.

Misail Anyuta Ivanovna. It's nice to see you. Take your coat off. Can we have some tea?

Anyuta No thank you. I'm not really making a call.

Misail No?

Cleopatra You met Papa in the street.

Anyuta Yes.

Misail I know – you are on your way to Madame Azhogina's. We'll go together. I haven't been there for weeks.

Anyuta They've asked me to take a part.

Misail But I thought you didn't approve.

Anyuta This is to be a *tableau vivant*. I am to play Glory.

Misail How splendid.

Anyuta I wish Cleo would come. But she says your father would not like it.

Misail Oh, he thinks it's all wrong. Why don't you risk it? He needn't find out.

Cleopatra I couldn't.

Misail You'd know lots of the people.

Anyuta I believe Dolzhikov's daughter will be there tonight.

Cleopatra We heard her piano.

Misail I've not met her. Will she take part?

Anyuta Oh no. We are not up to her standard, I'm afraid. She will just sit and watch us. I believe she spent a whole winter in a private opera in St Petersburg.

Cleopatra They say all her clothes are French.

Misail Well, if you're ready. Do I need a coat?

Cleopatra Anyuta?

Anyuta I didn't call to ask you to take me to Madame Azhogina's.

Misail No?

Anyuta No. Cleo is worried because you have lost your job. She asked me to persuade you to do what your father wants.

Misail I can't. She knows that.

Anyuta Well, if you won't go back to this job, let us help to find you another.

Misail There are no others.

Anyuta There must be.

Misail She knows that I must work. I don't know why or for what purpose the thirty thousand people in this town live, but I know I must work.

Cleopatra But that is exactly what Papa wants you to do.

Misail I mean work. I am ashamed at the way we live. At the useless waste and corruption. We live well on capital and official salaries and let the rest of the people scrape their living as best they can. The houses smell of beetroot soup. And on fast days they smell of fish. There is nothing. There is nothing. No theatre. No decent orchestra. The libraries are unused. There are no gardens for the children. The servants are treated to the condition of vermin. The drinking water is filthy and people, very rich people who squander away whole fortunes and estates on one wager, do nothing with it and drink the filthy water themselves because of their stupidity and their meanness and their lethargy. They all take bribes. My father and your father, Anyuta, and they think of it as part of their payment. People in trouble can't even get advice without paying for it. Last week the military commander's wife had so many drinks given to her by young officers currying favour that she had to be carried out of church blind drunk. And even if there was something else I could do, it would only be to set your minds at rest. My dears. It is only the girls in this town who have any compassion left in their hearts. Have any honesty. But they will not let them understand this life and cheat you into believing that their attitudes are moral. And when you marry, you grow old quickly and let go and sink in the mud of this town's vulgar small existence. Tell me, who has ever heard of us? In Kimry I know they make boots. In Tula, they make samovars. What about us? What are we for?

Pause.

Anyuta There is something you could do. They're opening a telegraph in Dubetchnya near the new railway. My father will talk to Dolzhikov.

Cleopatra You can work the telegraph, Misail. I know you can.

22

Anyuta Will you go and see Dolzhikov in the morning? I'll arrange it.

Cleopatra Misail?

Misail I hadn't thought of the railway.

Cleopatra And will you stop going to Madame Azhogina's for a little while anyway?

Misail I can't. They're starting a new play.

Anyuta I can explain.

Misail I was going to be the prompter.

She takes the script.

Anyuta I must go.

Cleopatra I'll come out with you.

They exit. Door bangs. Cleopatra re-enters.

Misail Dubetchnya is fourteen miles away. (*Pause.*) It's getting dark. The lamp needs oil. I'll fill it up.

SCENE TWO

Dubetchnya. In front of the manor house. It has been deserted for years. The sound of hammering comes from inside.
     Misail Alexandr and Ivan Cheprakov are looking at the house.

Misail Go back to the office, there's a good fellow. It is *your* turn.

Ivan Why are you always coming up to the house?

Misail Look, Ivan, there's nobody on duty. What if a message comes through?

Ivan What does it matter? No one will know.

Misail Who is working in there? I thought the house was still empty.

Ivan Moisey told Mama there would be workmen here soon. (*Pause.*) Flies. (*Pause.*) What a dreadful luncheon Mama gave us. Always milk soup and curd pies. She's so mean. Hang on.

He tries to catch a fly.

Misail Hello there.

Andrey Ivanov comes out of the house.

Andrey Ivanov!

Andrey Misail Alexandr! I thought it must be you.

Misail You don't know what it's like to see someone from town.

Andrey With God all things are possible. What are you doing here anyway?

Misail Ivan. This is someone from home. Andrey Ivanov.

Ivan A workman.

Andrey I am not a workman. I am a contractor.

Ivan You seem to have been working.

Misail Of course he's been working. He's a very fine workman. Why do you deny it, Andrey? You know how much you are in demand.

Andrey I am a contractor.

Misail You'd be better off if you worked by yourself.

Andrey I am a contractor. And now if you'll excuse me –

Ivan What are you doing in there?

Andrey The engineer has bought the house.

Misail Dolzhikov? Why?

Ivan Why? Because it's a very fine house. When Mama and my father the General lived in it, it was the best house in the whole province. I was born in there. Behind those shutters is the drawing room. I would come down and meet the guests.

That is why he bought it.

Andrey Dolzhikov bought it because he believes money is safer in land than in banknotes.

Ivan Hee. Hee. Mama would be pleased. Wait –

He catches a fly and eats it.

Andrey What did you do?

Ivan I catch flies and I eat them. But I find them rather sour. *Bonjour*, Monsieur.

He exits.

Andrey With God all things are possible.

Misail Sometimes he takes his clothes off and runs round the countryside naked. You know his mother?

Andrey The General's widow? I borrowed five roubles off her to pay the rent last year when we were working on your Telegraph Office. I'm still paying her back a rouble a month interest.

Misail Well, she talks and she eats, but there's something deathly about her. And the only thing that lights up in her is a glimmer of consciousness that she is an aristocrat and once owned serfs. Sometimes some of that flares up in him. But how are you? Have you been well?

Andrey Not too good. Just before we came out here. Whatever it is. I don't know. Here. That tries to eat me up. Anyway I was down with it and they thought I would go. Then one day I sat up in bed and felt a bit better. Anything can happen. Anything can change. I escaped again. With God all things are possible.

Misail Why are you out here alone?

Andrey The men are at the station. Tiling the roofs.

He lights his pipe.

Misail And you're working for the engineer. Here.

Andrey No. I work for the widow's bailiff.

Misail Moisey?

Andrey Yes. Dolzhikov is expected here to inspect the property. They want it to look in reasonable shape. I'm only doing it to pay off the interest. What wickedness one takes part in.

Misail Hard work?

Andrey Nothing. You?

Misail Hard. Ours is really nothing. You can hear the telegraph wires humming if you listen, but you have no more work than a child could do. Ivan and I generally leave the boy in the office. We chat with his mama, or I walk in the orchard. And think and talk to myself. Through there it has been cleared. The peasants pay Moisey for the grazing. Way down beyond it is a mill. Sometimes I go down there. I listen to the mill wheels working and it makes me depressed. I wish I was peaceful like the mill pond which is deep and full of fish. I think what sort of life is this for a grown man? Waiting for someone to send a telegram. I sit and wish I was back in town or feel bored or wish I could just fade away. Who helps you at Azhogina's now?

Andrey No one. I have to help myself. I thought you'd stopped coming there because of your father, and all the time you were out here.

Misail Did you perform the new play? I was going to be the prompter.

Andrey We've done another one since then. I did a great backdrop for her. Scenes from the mythology of Greece.

Misail Her daughters. Did they perform?

Andrey Oh yes. The three of them. Nymphs they were. I painted them a little waterfall.

Misail And were they very serious?

Andrey They looked more stern than Madame Mufke. And she gave us her Hecuba among the Trojan women.

Misail And I'm stuck out here.

Andrey Anything can happen. Anything can change.

Misail But it's when I most determine to change that I doubt myself the most. Did you walk to Dubetchnya from town?

Andrey How else?

Misail So did I. Listen. Sometimes I think such marvellous things and draw such brilliant conclusions but my thoughts are always broken by visions of rissoles or bowls of porridge. Madame Cheprakov feeds us so badly and it makes me realise why the peasant who scrabbles for bread all his life has no time to think of anything else. I can imagine if I had to work – I mean really work – that the poverty and desperation of the workman's life would be more than I could bear. If I could work – well, like Dolzhikov works, engineering, building, bringing this railway – it might be all right! But I couldn't. I used to dream of the intellectual life, and imagine myself a doctor or a writer or a teacher. But my dreams remain dreams. I like the theatre and reading. When I was younger they were a passion with me, but my mind has probably never known any real activity. In school I had such an aversion to the Greek language that they took me away in the fourth form and sent me to a tutor. It was no good. I still couldn't learn. And yet I like reading. The work I have done since I left school is nothing. It requires no effort. No talent. No creative impulse. I despise it, and I don't think for a moment that it justifies an idle, carefree life. It's nothing but a swindle and it brings a kind of wickedness itself.

Ivan calls in the distance.

Ivan Aiee. Poloznev.

Enter Ivan Cheprakov.

Poloznev, a carriage. Visitors.

Misail What?

Ivan Visitors.

Cleopatra (*calls off*) Misail. Misail Alexandr.

Misail My sister.

Andrey I must go inside.

Misail Please stay.

Andrey (*more callous*) No. I must go back to work.

Enter Cleopatra, Anyuta Blagovo and Dr Blagovo.

Misail Cleo.

Cleopatra We've come to take you for a picnic, but you're on duty I'm told.

Misail How did you get here?

Cleopatra The doctor hired a brake. Isn't that extravagant?

Doctor We called at the Telegraph Office and met this gentleman.

Misail You remember him, Cleo. Ivan Mikhailovich Cheprakov, may I introduce my sister, Cleopatra Alexandrovna.

Cleopatra He kissed my hand.

Misail Anyuta Ivanovna Blagovo.

Doctor Boris. Ivanovich.

Ivan How do you do?

Misail We've never met. You're in the army.

Cleopatra A doctor.

Ivan An army doctor.

Misail You're on leave.

Doctor Yes. From Kimry.

Cleopatra His family is in Petersburg.

Doctor Don't look for the wrinkles. I'm not an old man yet. I married in my second year at the university.

Cleopatra Where shall we have our picnic?

Misail I would like to take you down to the old mill, but I dare not go so far away.

Ivan Let's stay here.

Cleopatra We didn't invite him. Have we brought enough?

Doctor Look at the old house.

Ivan When we lived in it people used to pay calls in the summer, just like this. Everyone would sit out here. We would play games in front of the house and then come back to the veranda for refreshments.

Doctor What air. Holy Mother, what air. You should breathe, Cleopatra Alexine.

Cleopatra I do breathe.

They set out the picnic.

Doctor What a journey we had through the gardens. All those acres going to waste. There was an idiot standing in the orchard minding the cows. All the trees had to be propped up. They have grown so huge. You'd never believe they were just fruit trees.

Cleopatra Please, Anyuta, keep your eye on the time. We mustn't be late. Papa only let me come on condition I was at home again by six.

Ivan Oh, bother your papa.

Misail Cheprakov.

Doctor Here. Here. You will join us, *mon cher*.

They all sit.

This is pleasant. It is.

Ivan Penny Wise and I often sit out here and pretend.

Cleopatra Why does he call you that?

Ivan Half a loaf. Hee. Hee.

Cleopatra What does he mean?

Misail Nothing.

Ivan Hee. Hee.

Cleopatra Tell me.

Misail During the autumn term at school we used to catch goldfinches and linnets and sell them in the market early in the morning whilst our parents were still asleep. We watched for migrating starlings and fired at them with small shot. Some of them would die in terrible agony. I can remember their little cries in the cage at night. Those that recovered, we sold. Once I was left with only one starling. A cock bird. I couldn't get rid of it. In the end I managed to get a farthing for it. Anyway I said as I put the farthing in my pocket: half a loaf is better than no bread.

Ivan Hee. Hee.

Pause.

Doctor (*drinking his tea*) Ah. Now I know what bliss is. (*Walking about.*) How beautiful this country of ours is. So flat and green. And such air. Lucky Misail Alexandr out here.

Misail When do you go back to Kimry?

Doctor Next week. But I shall be back. Soon, I am going on an extended leave to Petersburg. To do some research.

Misail To your family? How many children have you got?

Doctor Two.

Misail Tell me. Do you like your work? Do you love your wife?

Doctor I married in my second year at the university. I love my work.

Cleopatra (*looking inside*) This room smells of mushrooms.

Misail Ivan Mikhailovich. One of us should go back to the office.

Ivan And I suppose because it is your family that is here it is I who should go. Well, I'll go to the office and see what's up and then I'll take Moisey's gun and go and shoot at the ducks, that's what I'll do. Mademoiselle. Doctor.

He exits.

Doctor An interesting case. (*To Misail.*) You're so serious. I like that in a man.

Cleopatra I don't ever want to go home. What a day.

Doctor What's that?

Misail Andrey Ivanov. You know, Anyuta, Madame Azhogina's scene painter.

Cleopatra I've seen him painting the church ceiling. He always looks so ill. Like a demon.

Doctor What does he complain of?

Misail I don't know. Sometimes he gets so ill. It is certain he will die. But he always recovers.

Doctor Shall we go inside?

Cleopatra Can we? I'm afraid.

Doctor Come on.

They go inside. Anyuta is packing the tea things. Misail helps her. Piano music comes from inside the house. Eventually Cleopatra comes running out.

Cleopatra I'm happy. I'm so happy. Is it possible?

She kisses Misail.

Misail Papa? How is he?

Cleopatra (*to Anyuta*) Oh, don't keep looking at your watch.

The Doctor comes out.

Doctor Well, ladies, if we are to please His Excellency the architect and make good time, we must consider leaving.

Misail Have you got everything?

Doctor Goodbye, Misail Alexyich. Take care out here. Lucky fellow.

Misail (*to Cleopatra*) Come on now. Don't cry. You looked so well today. So happy and pretty. Hasn't she looked pretty, Doctor? Tell Papa. Tell him. That all is well. I'll come down with you.

> *They exit. Pause. Andrey Ivanov comes out of the house. He lights a pipe. Then Dolzhikov comes out of the house, followed by Ivan Cheprakov.*

Dolzhikov There was only a boy on duty at the Telegraph Office. Why?

Ivan I'm sorry. I . . .

Dolzhikov I don't want your sorrow. I pay you. Why? You. Is that you working in there? Who contracted you to do that? Her ladyship? Getting things in order before we sign, is she? (*He laughs.*) They're not so stupid, these old ladies.

> *Enter Misail.*

You. You're the other fellow, are you? In a fortnight I'm transferring that office to the station. You'll have to pick your socks up there, my friends.

Ivan I do my best, your honour.

Dolzhikov Yes. I can see you do your best. (*At Misail.*) The best you lot can do is to take your salary. Always relying on the family to stop you getting the sack. Well, I don't care for patronage. No one took any trouble on my behalf. Before I got this railway contract, I worked. I didn't start life as an engineer either. I was a mechanic.

I've been a labourer. I've worked, I have. So it doesn't please me to find no one in that office. (*To Andrey.*) What are you doing still here? I suppose you all drink together. (*To Ivan.*) Come on, you. I want to send some telegrams. I haven't much time. There's a carriage waiting to take me back to town.

Dolzhikov and Ivan Cheprakov exit. Pause.

Andrey Was that the goddess Glory with your sister?

Misail And her brother. Do you know, Anyuta didn't speak a word to me. She's a wonderful girl. A wonderful girl. My sister was so happy. Like a child. But she got into the carriage as if it was a scaffold. (*Pause.*) Andrey Ivanov. Take me on. Let me work for you.

Andrey What?

Misail Please, Andrey. Let me work for you. Take me on.

Andrey I must get my things.

Misail I want to go home.

Andrey I must go down to the men on the line. Dolzhikov will want to inspect the work, I should think. He nearly had a strike on his hands last time we were out here. With the navvies. He dealt with it though. He laid all the men off. And when they became desperate, he welcomed them back with open arms but at two-thirds their normal rate of pay. Things are better for them now. But they behave themselves. This railway won't ever reach the town because the town won't pay him his bribe of 50,000 roubles to take it there. So because of the town's meanness and his avarice, the nearest station will remain where it is, four miles outside. Misail, our good angel. Vermin consumes the crop, rust consumes iron, and cheating, cheating consumes the soul. God have mercy on us all.

Andrey Ivanov has been contracted to convert some houses into a shop. Misail is wheeling rubble from inside and dumping it outside. The men are barefoot. Dusty. Andrey Ivanov and a Workman are with the Shopkeeper.

Workman Looks as if it's going to be like this all day, your honour.

Shopkeeper What do you say?

Workman I say it's going to be hot all day.

Shopkeeper It'll rain later I shouldn't wonder.

Workman You're quite right. Looks as if it might cloud over later. Look at that.

Andrey signals him away.

Andrey Do you want to see inside, sir?

Shopkeeper No. How long are you going to be?

Andrey I reckon if this weather continues we'll be clear by tomorrow and we can start repairing the roof and then the shelves and the counter can go up.

Shopkeeper Well, whatever the weather decides to do, I want this ready when I arranged for it to be ready or you'll be looking to someone else for payment. I've already got too much stuff from the warehouse stored on my other premises. I shall want to be moving things here next week.

Andrey I should think that ought to be all right, sir.

Shopkeeper It had better be.

Andrey You won't mind me asking, sir. But about the fee. We arranged, I think I'm right in saying, that once I'd

35

started work you'd give me a third of the fee down, so I can get materials and pay the men.

Shopkeeper Did we?

Andrey Ay, we did. If that's all right.

Shopkeeper Let's see how far you've got by tomorrow, shall we? I'll be back then.

Andrey I think I can manage till then.

Misail enters carrying bricks.

Shopkeeper Right. I'd better just have a glance inside. I see you're dumping quite a bit. I hope it's nothing I could use. I bought those houses' fixtures and fittings. What's he doing now?

Andrey Just clearing the bricks.

Shopkeeper Who is he?

Andrey One of my men.

Shopkeeper One of your men, is he? I know you. What are you doing here? I don't want that scoundrel working for me.

Andrey He's not working for you, sir. He's working for me.

Shopkeeper It amounts to much the same. I'm paying.

Andrey Not yet, sir.

Shopkeeper He'll bring talk on my business. I don't like that.

Andrey No, sir. But he's a good labourer. I shan't dismiss him.

Shopkeeper Won't you now?

Andrey No, sir.

36

Shopkeeper I don't like his sort. It won't look good. You'll lay him off directly.

Andrey No, sir. It's good weather. I doubt that it will last. There's plenty of work to be contracted at the moment.

Shopkeeper Call yourself a contractor. Where's your ethics? You want to quit now, do you?

Andrey I didn't say I was quitting, sir. As long as I can pay the men and employ my own workers. This suits me fine.

Workman And we shall need paying tomorrow. I can tell you that.

Shopkeeper (*to Misail*) It's not you I care about, you blackguard. It's your father. What a precious fool he must feel. In his position. Right. You get on with it as you feel like.

Andrey Ivanov bows.

You, don't you loaf.

The Workman bows.

You. I should like to see you locked up. You bloody scoundrelly fool. I'll be here in the morning. I shall expect work done.

He exits. They laugh.

Andrey (*to the Workman*) You, don't you loaf.

Another Workman Never mind, Misail Alexandrovich. They wouldn't know. They wouldn't understand a man like you. A man of religion.

They work.
Presently Doctor Blagovo and Maria Viktorovna Dolzhikova come down the street.

Maria Is not that he?

Doctor Misail Alexandr.

Maria Hello.

Doctor We thought we'd take a spin in the carriage. But we've left it in the square and come down here on foot, to see you at it. Maria Viktorovna Dolzhikova, may I present Misail Alexandr?

Maria You have become quite a figure, Monsieur Poloznev.

Misail Not for long I hope. (*Pause.*) My hands.

Maria I don't care about that.

She takes his hand.

You must forgive me. I've been told so much about you. The doctor is in love with you. You seem to be the only interesting native of this dreadful place. Is that rude? It's hot, is it not?

Misail It's hot work. Thirsty. The plaster gets in your throat. You want to drink. But it's as healthy as it's likely to get. The weather I mean.

Doctor We're meeting my sister in the Italian café at four. Won't you come? Slake it.

Misail I *am* employed, you know. And I hardly could. Could I? Like this.

Maria We hope your sister will be there. I asked the doctor to make me acquainted with you both. I have no friends here. I watch for you both out of my sitting-room window. Your sister has such a kind look of concentration. I see her walking in the evening with your papa. I haven't seen you at all, lately.

Doctor How are you finding the working man's life, old chap?

Misail Much as you would expect, I suppose. Hard. When I get home in the evening after work, I fall asleep over my meal. I can't go out again. I sleep. Then it's time for work again. But I'm very happy. It's made my life easier. It's set me free of doubt.

Maria What do you mean by that, I wonder?

Misail I feel as if I had been born again. And I can do. Well. Anything I want. Everything interests me. I can sleep during our dinner hour. Lying on the ground against the wall on the building site. I can go about barefoot. I can stand in a queue at the shop. In a crowd. A cab horse fell in his shafts yesterday. I could run and help without being afraid of soiling my clothes or feel . . . I'm sorry. I must get back to work.

Maria Why don't I see you in Great Dvoryansky Street these last few weeks? You didn't say.

Misail I'm not living at home any more.

Maria You have another apartment?

Misail I've moved. I'm staying with our old nurse, Karpovna. In Makarikha Prospect.

Maria I see. Will you dine with me later this week? Now that we have met. I should like to, well, see you again. Boris?

Doctor I'd love to. Count me in. Sponger. You know me. Misail?

Misail I must get back. Our foreman is looking for me.

Maria We won't keep you.

Doctor Shall we give your regards to our sisters when we see them?

Misail Please do.

Maria You will come, won't you? My father is out of town at the moment. I know so few people. It would be very nice.

He bows. They go. The men whistle.

Andrey Misail Alexandr. Since you became a nine days' wonder. My business is suffering.

Misail Forgive me, Andrey. I didn't intend to stop.

Workman You're doing all right there, Misail. For a man of principle.

Andrey You get on with that.

Workman You watch it. We haven't been paid yet, if you remember.

Anyuta comes down the street.

Andrey Here comes the goddess Glory. Going to tea at this time I should think. Don't be long.

Misail Anyuta. (*Pause.*) Anyuta. I mustn't stop. Boris and Mademoiselle Dolzhikova have gone to the Italian café.

Anyuta Please don't talk to me in the street. If this is necessary for you, all right. As it should be. But. But then. Please. Don't acknowledge me. In the street. Please don't speak to me.

She's crying.
She exits. He goes on working.

*A tavern. Misail and the Doctor have just finished a game
of billiards. The Doctor is wearing a silk shirt. Smoking
and drinking. In another room a concertina is playing.
An Old Man is sitting watching them.*

Misail Let's have another game.

Doctor No. No. You're the champion. Let's have another
drink.

Misail plays alone.

Talk. Let us talk. Can't we talk?

Misail stops.

This is the only place worth going to in this whole town,
and you, my dear chap, are the only man worth talking
to. True. You don't know how strange it was among all
the dead creatures that are washed up here to find
someone actually living among all those pig-faces. Shake
hands.

Misail Drink, Doctor. Drink.

Doctor No. No. Shake hands. You're a good man, Misail
Alexandr. But truly. Listen. Tell me. The fight you have
put up. The odds you fought against. The effort it must
have cost you to act as you have. Really – the, well, don't
you feel – Doesn't it leave you feeling you wished such
energy had gone into something else? A career. Art.
Science. Don't you feel that?

Misail No.

Doctor You don't drink. No. Seriously? The – well,
damn it, the spiritual torment. Was it worth it? Well.
Frankly. For what you do?

Misail The strong should not enslave the weak. A minority should not live like vermin off the lives of the rest. Everyone should take his own part in the struggle for existence. And I can see no better way for me of equalling the struggle than by means of the work I do, with my hands.

Doctor Then do you think that everyone without exception ought to engage in manual labour in the form of a universal service, compulsory for all?

Misail I do.

Doctor But listen, old chap. If everyone spent his time taking part equally in the struggle for existence, what would happen to the future?

Misail It would still be there, I suppose.

Doctor No, Poloznev. Just tell me, if you please, what would happen if all the scientists, all the men of ideas, all the engineers, gave up their work to help build the bridges they'd designed or had to dig the canals or till the fields or whatever. What would happen?

Misail Look, Doctor. I understand your argument. I appreciate it. But it is used as a defence of our new kind of slavery. We may have freed the peasant but have we not enslaved the worker? We may think it outmoded to beat our servants. But we still have servants. The forms of inequality may change, they don't disappear. There is no desire for it.

Doctor There is no desire for equality. That's human nature, I suppose. What time is it? Are you meeting your sister tonight?

Misail No.

Doctor I thought you were. She was at our house today. Come on, let us play.

They play.

I suppose it is an expression of the will to survive.

Misail I cannot see any point in survival on the present terms.

Doctor But damn it all, that's nonsense. What about progress? If the snail withdraws into its shell, do you call that progress? That's all you want when it comes down to it. A kind of personal sanctity. Progress is infinite. What you want is to restrict progress for the freedom of what? Forgive me. But look, I am on a ladder. I am going up. I don't know where. I am going to work. Yes, work. *That* is work. In Petersburg I am going to study. Because I must find out what is there. What you want is that we should impede progress and contemplate provincial life, for the better harmony of all our souls. What do I know about slavery? If insects devour one another, let them. I can't help it. There is the future. I will help define it.

Misail I don't want to be sacrificed to a non-existent future in the name of progress.

Doctor The world will progress.

Misail Not necessarily without direction.

Doctor With or without it. It depends on what you mean by direction.

Misail Or progress.

Doctor Words.

Misail I agree. Let us play again. Listen, Doctor. That we must work *now* is what I think. For now. We must not ignore something actual in defence of something that does not exist. Or think that we are licensed by the future to do what we like in the present. It's all very well to talk about progress in that abstract way, but I really believe

43

that if in order to define your future you thought that a way could be found to hand one of your more unpleasant physiological functions on to the working class, then I think you would try and arrange it.

The Old Man laughs.

Doctor You liked that, didn't you, Grandpa? If you could shit for us and we wanted you to, you'd let us.

Cleopatra is in the street outside. A Workman has been pissing against the wall. She asks him something. He comes in.

Workman Misail Alexandrovich. A lady to see you.

Misail What?

Workman She's outside.

Misail Doctor –

Doctor Hang on. I'll get into my coat.

Misail goes out.

Here you are, Grandpa. Finish it.

Gives him the bottle. Misail is outside.

Misail Cleopatra, what are you doing here? How did you find a place like this?

Cleopatra I called at Karpovna's. Prokofy told me you might be here.

Doctor Good evening, Cleopatra Alexine.

Cleopatra Good evening, Boris.

Doctor Let's not stop here. You'll freeze. Shall we go to my father's house? No. I suppose not.

Misail I have to be up at five. We're starting a new job.

Doctor What doing?

Misail Mending the roof of the Literary Club. At least it will be indoors for a while. Why did you come here, Cleo? Does Father know you're out?

Cleopatra No. He's ill.

Misail Father?

Cleopatra Yes. But he won't rest. He's gone to the club, so I came out. I wanted you to know.

Misail That's good of you.

Cleopatra I know you must obey your conscience, but can't you do it differently so as not to annoy Papa?

Pause.

Doctor Well, we can't stay here all night.

Cleopatra I must get back soon. Father will wonder where I am.

Misail Then why did you come out in the first place?

Doctor I'll take you home. Misail Alexandr?

Misail Thank you.

The Doctor and Cleopatra exit.

Goodnight.

SCENE FIVE

Maria Viktorovna, the Doctor and Misail Alexandr are dining at Dolzhikov's house.

Doctor Maria Viktorovna, Maria Victrix! You've got him to drink.

He raises his glass.

45

Maria Would you like some more, Doctor?

Doctor I would. I am afraid I would, my dear.

Misail The meal was splendid.

Maria Oh, I am glad. I didn't think you were enjoying it.

She fills the Doctor's glass.

Shall we go into the other room?

Doctor No. No. It's so nice in here.

Maria I thought you could play for us.

Doctor No, let us stay in here.

Maria Do you mind?

Misail This is so pleasant.

Doctor Besides, I shan't play unless you sing for us.

Misail Do you sing?

Doctor Does she sing? Old chap, don't say it. Does she sing?

Maria I hardly sing at all nowadays.

Misail Why is that?

Maria I haven't the desire. Doctor, would you like one of Papa's cigars? Imported.

Doctor The engineer would be furious.

Maria No. Here, I'll light it.

Doctor You don't offer one to my friend.

Maria I know he doesn't smoke.

Misail No.

Doctor Now talk. Talk is better than cards. Maria. You

shall begin. You were about to say what you thought of our friend's new life? Let us continue. Continue.

Maria All the evil in our life comes from idleness, I think.

Doctor Ye–es.

Maria Boredom and a spiritual poverty is inevitable when one is accustomed to living at other people's expense. The rich and well educated ought to work like everyone else and if there is comfort it ought to be available to all. There surely ought not to be a world so full of privilege for so few people. I tell you it is not pleasant to be rich.

Doctor Make to yourself friends of the Mammon of unrighteousness, it says.

Maria And truly. For there cannot be a Mammon and justice. Comfort and luxury have a magical power. Little by little they seduce even the strongest of wills. Once upon a time Father and I lived simply. But now you see how. It is something monstrous. We spend twenty thousand a year. In the provinces!

Doctor Monstrous.

Maria It is.

Misail But though your father is rich, yet he has worked for it, he says.

Maria He likes to talk like a workman too. Even in society. It's a fancy, a whim. Like my education in France or my year at the Petersburg Conservatoire. Only that his having worked with his hands makes his money seem more honestly got. Talented, richly endowed, imaginative natures know what to do in our situation. Know what to do with their lives. They show the way. So that mediocre people like me can follow. We can sense from them that there are deeper currents moving in our society and we float while they carry us.

Doctor How can you sense from anyone what does not exist? There is no end to what the new wave of writers would have us believe. They have invented intellectual workers in the country and you may search through the villages till you're blue in the face and find at the most one complaining lout in a reefer jacket who will make four mistakes spelling a word with three letters. Or if you are fortunate you may find some good man like our Misail who, fleeing from his heritage in the middle class, will do us the service of pretending to be what he is not and convince us that things may be changing for the better after all. A real change is not to be found anywhere in this whole huge country. There is the same savagery, the same uniform boorishness, the same hopelessness as there was five hundred years ago. With the upper classes still wandering around in the ridiculous maze of Peter the Great's table of ranks. We are told that the beginning of Russia was 852. The beginning of civilised Russia is not even in sight. Social movements there have been. And all they have left us is a chaos that is being exploited, my dear Maria, by men like your father out for what they can get, and the future will be dictated largely by them. It is this railway that is the current *we* shall be carried by. Meanwhile we must study and study and study and wait until we are mature and then put our findings to use.

Maria Goodness, how tiresome you are lately. Have you nothing of the woman in you, Doctor? You cannot be so without intuition.

Doctor My dear lady, the happiness of mankind in the future lies only in techniques. I drink to science.

Maria Well, there is no doubt about one thing. One has to organise one's life somehow differently. Life as it has been until now is not worth having. So let us change the subject.

Doctor Don't you love her? Isn't she splendid?

Maria Be quiet. Go and get my album. It's through there. I want to make a sketch.

Doctor *Enchanté.*

He kisses her hand and exits.

Maria Dear Doctor. How grateful I am to him. If it wasn't for him you wouldn't come here. Isn't that so? Some coffee?

Misail Please.

Maria What do you think of him?

Misail The doctor? I like him. Really I suppose he is the first well-educated man I have ever met in my whole life. I cannot judge whether he really knows a great deal, but at least he shares what he knows with the rest of us and when he talks about anything to do with medicine he is not like any of the other doctors in town, and I fancy that if he liked he might really become a man of science. He makes me feel how ridiculous it is to have so little knowledge of the actual world. I do not know for example what the oil or the paints I work with are made up of. That's ridiculous, isn't it? When I know so much that is of no use. He lives by argument. And that is good because although I usually remain of the same opinion, yet, thanks to him, I begin to try and see what I am doing and why, so that everything shall become clear in my mind.

Maria Is he really so perfect?

Misail I don't know about that. He may be the best and most cultivated man in town, but in his manner of constantly turning every conversation into a debate, there is something coarse, rather like a divinity student, and when he takes off his coat and sits in his silk shirt or flings down a tip to a waiter in a restaurant I feel that cultured he may certainly be, but that the Tartar is fermenting in him still.

Maria What a dear you are.

The Doctor enters.

Doctor Here we are.

Maria Thank you. Coffee?

Doctor My dear lady. It's nearly two. If I leave you so soon, will I be forgiven?

Maria Why is that?

Doctor I see I am late, I have an appointment.

Maria So late?

Doctor So late. You must sketch our friend. Poloznev. You'll forgive me. Maria Viktorovna, more of this before I leave next week.

Maria Indeed. I'll call for Pavel.

Doctor No. I'll let myself out. *Bonsoir*. My greatcoat is in the hall.

Maria Goodnight, Doctor.

Exit Doctor.

Help yourself. I'm going to put you in my book. Tell me about your work. I've had enough philosophising for one evening. Tell me something amusing. Is it true that you spend on yourself only what you earn? Tell me a story. You must have a story.

Misail I don't know what amuses you, but I'll tell you something that happened to me yesterday. We finished a job papering a reading room in my father's club. We did three rooms altogether and it was arranged that we should be paid piecework at a rate of seven copecks. When we had finished I went to the office to draw the wages and I was given a chit to sign, even though they were only giving us the seven, which said that the rate we were being paid at was twelve copecks. Of course I refused to sign and they wouldn't give me the money. I was dealing with one of the committee – an old man with gold spectacles. He threatened to knock me down, but a servant whispered to him that I was an architect's son just in time for him to recover himself. So I drew the money and signed for the correct amount and he scowled and I paid the men and came away.

Maria How terrible. I've nearly finished. Do they always treat you like that?

Misail Oh yes. It's always like that. You do the job and then you have to go to the back door for your wages, cap in hand like a beggar.

Maria There. Look. You must inscribe it. What is the matter? Don't you like it? It's not very good. Why are you so quiet? What are you thinking?

Misail Only that you treat me very kindly. Rather as you might a poor old dog that has been kicked out by its owners. When you tire of me will you turn me out of doors again?

Maria If that is how it appears. It is not my fault. Give it to me, please. Perhaps you want to hurt me because you are not happy with your life after all? Is that not so?

Misail How do you mean?

Maria Well, look how careful you are to change when you come here. Tell me, isn't that odd for someone with such conviction? Look at what it is that you have chosen to do. Painting, decorating, mending roofs. Surely that does not satisfy you? Serving the rich. Is that what you mean when you tell us we should work for our bread by the sweat of our brows? You work for money and not for bread. Why have you not kept to your word? You should be in the field. You should be ploughing and sowing and reaping. Don't look at me. I know what you think of me. Drawing and singing and leading such a life. But I know. Look *here*. Let me show you.

She goes to the cupboard and returns with an armful of books.

Voilà. This is my secret. This is my estate. Here I have fields and a kitchen garden. An orchard. A dairy. Beehives. Look. I study. I know all they have to tell me. Here you see. My notebook. My accounts. What crops in what rotation. My dream it is to start a new life. To go to our Dubetchnya in March as soon as spring is here. It's marvellous there in Dubetchnya, is it not? My father has promised to give me the estate and I shall do with it exactly as I please. At first I shall be careful and only plan and make ready and think what will be for the best. But then in the second year I shall work. I shall work. Really work. Do you not long for the country? I long for a change. Don't be angry with me. When the doctor goes, I shall have no one here but you. Until the spring comes, and then I shall go into the country. Oh, let it come.

SCENE SIX

Karpovna's house. Prokofy eating his supper. Karpovna dozing. A light burning in front of icons. Misail in his room.

Prokofy Mama, you have been good to me.

Karpovna Ay.

Prokofy I will show you a testimony of my affection. All this life I will cherish you. In your declining years in this vale of tears I will care for you and when you die I will bury you at my expense. I have said it and you can believe it. (*Eats.*)

Karpovna Ay. Ah.

Prokofy Is it bad?

Karpovna Ay.

Prokofy I should try a drop of this.

Karpovna Nay. Holy Mother. That would never do.

In his room Misail is cold. He puts his book down and comes into the room. Prokofy stumbles to his feet.

Prokofy Misail Alexandr.

Karpovna Are you cold, angel?

Misail No. I'm all right.

Prokofy It's warmer in here.

Karpovna Sit.

Prokofy No work?

Misail No.

Prokofy Not the season.

Misail You?

Prokofy Always something for a butcher. Gech! (*He chops the table with his hand.*) Some people always eat. Thank the Lord.

Misail I tried to get work on the railway this morning.

Prokofy No go?

Misail We started to mend a roof down there yesterday. The weather stopped us. Then we had trouble with the navvies.

Prokofy Fists?

Misail Ay.

Prokofy Have some soup.

Misail Thank you. (*Pause. He eats.*) Have you no idea, nurse, who sent those books today, and this scarf?

Karpovna No, my dear. A maidservant brought them in a parcel and she wouldn't say who she was from.

Misail It smells of lilies of the valley. Doesn't it?

Prokofy Ay.

Prokofy pushes the glass towards Misail.

Have some.

Karpovna He doesn't drink. Ay. Ay.

Misail What is it, nurse?

Karpovna My ear. It's aching.

Misail I'm sorry.

Karpovna Do you want some more?

Misail Please.

Karpovna Holy saints in heaven. Your life is ruined. There will be trouble.

Prokofy gets up.

Misail You off?

Prokofy Ay.

Karpovna Don't be late.

Prokofy No, my dear.

Exits. The old woman sleeps. Misail eats. Goes to his room. It is cold. Front door bangs. Enter Cleopatra. She is cold.

Misail Cleo.

He kisses and embraces her.

Nurse, it's Cleopatra Alexyina.

Cleopatra coughs.

My dear, you look awful.

Karpovna What a colour.

Cleopatra hasn't moved.

Misail You shouldn't have come out. You'll catch a chill. Give me your things.

He goes out. The nurse gets her a drink. Misail comes back in. Takes her coat. Exits.

Karpovna Warm yourself.

Cleopatra (*suddenly*) Nurse, what have I been doing until now? Tell me. I've wasted my youth. All the best years of my life, to know nothing but keeping accounts. Pouring tea. Counting the halfpennies. Thinking there was nothing better in the world. As though I was dreaming. I want to live. I am human. I am. They have turned me into a housekeeper.

She flings the bunch of keys on her belt on to the floor and goes into Misail's room.

Give me my things.

Misail What's the matter? You're unhappy. Is it me? Tell me.

Cleopatra I love him. I love him. He's gone to Petersburg. I'm frightened. I was happy. I love him. I love him. It's all right. Please. Leave me alone.

She goes to the nurse, picks up the keys. Kisses her.

You must forgive me, nurse. Something odd has been happening to me lately.

She exits.

SCENE SEVEN

Karpovna's house. Misail is at the table, eating. Karpovna is in her chair.

Karpovna Are you going to the engineer's this evening?

Misail No.

Karpovna How's that?

Misail I haven't been there for a week. I've sold my serge trousers.

Karpovna Will you be working tomorrow?

Misail I don't know. I hope so. Where's Prokofy?

Karpovna He'll be in. Some more tea?

Misail Please.

Karpovna You've sold your nice new trousers. Are they not pleased with you?

Misail Who?

Karpovna At the engineer's.

Misail Nurse. Please leave me alone.

Karpovna The samovar was humming this morning. There'll be trouble, you mark my words.

Pause.

Misail I went to Great Dvoryansky Street yesterday.

Karpovna Did you speak to your father?

Misail I hid in the garden and watched the house. I saw Father come home from the club. Cleo came to the door with a lamp, plaiting her hair with one hand. Then he went into the front room. Father was talking and Cleo sat in the armchair, not listening but thinking. Then they went upstairs. And the lights went out. I went across to the engineer's house and looked through the window but there was no one there. It was raining and dark. I felt lonely and cold. The actions and desires of the living are of no consequence compared to their miseries. I pulled the Dolzhikovs' bell – hard – so that it broke. I ran down the street like a naughty boy. I thought someone would be sure to come out and see who it was, but no one did. Thank you.

He goes to his room. The nurse sleeps. Misail prays. Eventually the front door bangs. He goes out and comes back with Maria.

Maria Since you won't come to me, I have to come to you. Why have you stopped calling on me? Why? (*Pause.*) Don't desert me. I'm so lonely. Your sister is always at home now and I never see her and Mademoiselle Blagovo hates me for some reason. I am alone in this awful place and I have no one but you. Don't desert me.

She cries. He kisses her.

SCENE EIGHT

Dubetchnya. Misail Alexandr and Maria in the fields.

Maria Your father came this morning.

Misail My father?

Maria He came in a carriage. Making a call. I sent him away.

Misail You shouldn't have done that.

Maria Why shouldn't I?

Misail It's a long way for him to come.

Maria He's gone anyway. (*Pause.*) I thought it was the best thing to do. (*Pause.*) I don't care.

Misail I do. (*Pause. He calls.*) Grigori. How are you? How are you doing? Time to eat. To eat. Can't hear.

Maria Here it is. Timothy grass. As high as me where you haven't cut it. How big, how far. (*Pause.*) I've been working today. The peasants don't seem overjoyed, I must say. But I've had that old man from the village up. He says that he'll get the labour. We must get it finished before the autumn or it will take another year. We should be all right, I think.

Misail Yes.

Maria They need a school.

Misail I hate the country.

Maria You can't.

Misail I do.

Maria You mustn't.

Misail I hate it. I do.

Maria You mustn't. Misail!

Misail I don't. I love it. But I'm wrong for it. You shouldn't have sent him away.

Maria Don't say that.

Misail I do say it.

Maria But one must be consistent in what one does.
I sent him away. I'm going to build that school. I am. It's
going to be built. It is. You'll see.

Misail You say that like a sledge driver on the high road
warning everyone to keep out of his way.

Maria I'm glad I do. So I should do. My grandfather was
a sledge driver. We don't spring fully armed from the
table of ranks in our family. My grandfather made his
money in Moscow when the French left. He bought up
a lot of surplus goods cheap and sold them again later for
a profit. He started life near Kiev, one of one hundred
and fifty serfs owned by a Count Ramiulin. He drove for
them. But he was a man of resources. And business. And
he did some trading with his sled on the quiet. He earned
enough to buy his freedom. One thousand roubles. He
was a valuable property, you see. He walked to Moscow
and made his money, as I have said. The family lived in
Kiev still. He bought them all off one by one. And died
one year before the repeal of the bond of servitude. He
had five sons. There was not a lot of money when it was
divided. My father travelled with his portion. He worked.
He says he is like his father and so am I too in some
ways. I despise these people fading away out here. My
father employs two thousand men.

Misail More than the Count owned.

Maria Grigori is leaning on his scythe. Why doesn't he
stop and eat? Stop . . . Eat. They are such fools sometimes.

SCENE NINE

*Dubetchnya. Inside the house. Misail is in an armchair.
Ivan Cheprakov, lighting a cigarette and drinking, is
dressed in the uniform of a railway guard.*

Ivan Do you know my life is impossible to imagine, it's so bad.

Misail Is it?

Ivan It's all right for you here. It's fine for you. Oh, I know I have a good job, but the worst of it is that any subaltern can shout, 'Hey, you guard,' and I can say nothing back. But I like trains. I overhear all sorts of things, and do you know I have learnt that life is a beastly thing. A doctor sat with me in my compartment the other day, and do you know he told me that if parents have been immoral, then their children become drunkards? Did you know that?

Misail I must wash and change. My feet. My back. Don't have any more, Ivan.

Ivan My mother has been the ruin of me.

Misail I'm so tired.

Ivan She has been the ruin of me.

Misail Ivan.

Ivan She has. Why haven't you gone down to the school? Isn't it the inauguration today?

Misail It is. But I had too much to do in the fields. At least, that is what I said. My father-in-law has come for the opening. I didn't want to be there. I made an excuse.

Ivan Will he come here?

Misail Yes.

Ivan I must go. (*He pours another drink.*)

Misail I don't know what to say to him. Where shall we put him? When we first came here, there was no furniture in the house at all, except for a piano and a child's armchair in the attic, so I sealed it off through there.

I decorated these rooms myself. It's the only work I like doing. We're ploughing again. I dream of ploughed land at night. I get up at dawn these days. I get worn out. The rain and the wind makes my face burn. I'm worn out. But I don't feel content. I don't understand farming. I have no feeling for it. I was so happy when we first came here, the happiest I can ever remember being. In the beginning, before we were married, I lived here like a hermit, making things ready for her. I worked hard. It was the winter and I was impatient for the spring and thinking it would never come. I used to walk through the snow to look for signs of the ice breaking on the river and as if in answer to my prayers it came early. And the floods came rushing down like a miracle. Then I used to walk out in the spring sunshine to meet her carriage when she came to see how I was doing. Sometimes, I walked so far to meet her that you could see the town in the distance and I wondered then what people made of us. We were married at Easter in the village church. Only Cleo came. We didn't ask my father. She said that Anyuta Ivanovna sent us her good wishes and of our marriage that God had sent me a new trial. There was only one priest and Maria drove us home in a little cart for all the world like a peasant woman. And we were so happy living here together planting in the garden and making our meals together. And in the evenings talking about our lives before we met. And she would cry when I told her about my father and yet how much I loved him and how much I wished things were not as they were between us. But then we had to face what we had taken on with the estate . . . I am from the town and I see the country from the town point of view. I love nature, the beauty of the sky, the fields. But not the work on them. It doesn't suit me. Then when we built the school. All the cheating and the bribes and your mother's man Moisey often behind the petty squabbles. The peasant who turns the soil with his plough and urges on his pitiful horse with his neck pushed forward into the rain. It's coarse. It's ugly. Savage. I think of life before the use of fire. It frightens me. The fierce bull that runs with the peasant's herd and the horses that they drive loose through the village. Everything – whether it's the ram or gander or the dogs in the yard. It all expresses the same force. And now in this weather the clouds hang over the fields. It frightens me.

Ivan Moisey is my mother's lover, I know it. He's a beastly man.

Misail Listen to the wind. Oh my wife. My wife. When she's not here. When she goes to town, as she does more and more now. This house. These rooms. This place. Everything about it, the garden, the yard, the trees, the horses in the stable. Everything that seems good when she is here makes me feel more alone when she is away. I sit at her desk for hours then. Among her books, listening to the clock and watching the night come black as soot to the windows. Or I take her gloves from a drawer and brood over them or the pen she keeps the accounts with or the little scissors in her workbasket. Everything I have done here is only because she wanted it. If she set me to cleanse a deep well I should do it without a thought. But this place of itself means nothing to me. The banging shutters, the squalor, the thieving. Without her it's like chaos. Hopeless, useless. I am not suited to life here. What happiness it is to love and be loved and how sad it is when you must leave the golden world. The fate of her library on farming is waiting for me. Our meeting, our marriage, are only episodes of which there will be many in the life of such a woman. All the best in the world is at her service and she takes it as her due. Ideas in vogue serve for her recreation. New intellectual fashions give variety to her life. I am only a sledge driver taking her from one entertainment to another. She does not need me. She is like a green parrot that had escaped and used to fly in the gardens of a square where I used to work.

Ivan I'm going home.

Pause. The door bangs. Enter Dolzhikov and Maria carrying parcels of wine and savouries.

Maria What weather. We should be putting the storm shutters in, Misail.

Misail How did it go?

Dolzhikov Here's my son-in-law in his working clothes. How are you then?

Misail Did it go all right?

Dolzhikov I think so. I'd say it did. It's a very tidy little place. Wouldn't you say so?

Misail No hitches?

Dolzhikov No. Some of the men were drunk. But the roof was finished.

Maria Only just.

Misail That's the main thing.

Maria Oh, they're such fools. I'm sick of them. What do they need a school for? They don't want it.

Dolzhikov She's tired.

Maria They don't. They'd rather have a bucket of vodka to shove at, like beasts at a trough.

Misail You see the marks on the window, but not what the window has to show. My father-in-law drinks and the doctor and Ivan. Look.

Dolzhikov Well, as no one asks me and there is no servant, I shall take my own coat off.

Misail Did the rain keep off?

Dolzhikov Yes it did. You were lucky there. It started on our way home.

Maria The villagers were holding candles and singing 'Holy Mother Our Redeemer'. The old man, Tit Petrov, gave me this. It's a salt cellar and he said, 'If anything has been said that shouldn't have been said or anything done that is not to your liking, forgive us.' Poor old man. It's built now, it's open. I'm so tired. I must go up. Give Papa some vodka, Misail. Look at what he's brought us. We must eat.

She exits.

Dolzhikov She's always like that after one of her escapades. It's a whim. A fancy. She did something of the sort before. She left me to become an opera singer. It took me two months to find her. I spent a thousand roubles on telegrams alone. You're a strange customer, I must say. You really are. This school. It's very good. It's a good idea. It is. But look at these people. Why don't you help the sick? Visit the imprisoned? You know what I mean. This lot. Peasants. I know them, man. They're not worth it. It's not poverty that's their trouble. You say it's poverty. It's not poverty. They're not men. They're frauds. Give me a workman any day. He understands. And the rich peasant is no different. He ill treats his children the same as the rest of them. There's the same mouth on him. And when he's had one too many he falls where he is and sleeps like the rest of them. Where's the furniture here? There used to be pictures. There used to be vases. There used to be lovely furniture in the Empire style. I bought the place with the furniture. You – (*To Ivan.*) You ought to know about this. Where is the furniture?

Ivan Moisey says that you bought the house but not the furniture. He had it moved.

64

Dolzhikov Moisey. Who's Moisey? I'll give him Moisey! You go and tell him that. Go on. Moisey. Shoo. Off you go. What are you hanging about in here for?

He growls at Ivan. Ivan exits.

There is no disputing, you are all naive, charming people, but for some reason as soon as you take to work, or go in for saving the peasants, in the long run you all go a bit odd. You don't drink. Now that's odd. I've brought one or two things. These are for Maria. I knew she'd like them. Fashion pictures. I'll go up. I didn't bring Pavel. You wrote about the shortage of space.

Dolzhikov exits. Misail alone.

Misail I must put my boots away.

Enter Ivan.

Ivan Where's he gone?

Misail Upstairs.

Ivan Shall I tell you? I know where all that furniture is. Upstairs in my mother's house. All of it. Crowded. Moisey had it moved.

Misail Go away, Ivan. My wife will be down in a minute. You know what she thinks.

Ivan takes the bottle.

Oh, leave that.

Ivan exits. Enter Maria.

Maria Autumn. Autumn. Autumn. Nothing green except the willows. It will be wet until it snows. Oh God. What are we doing here?

Misail Look at what your father has brought.

Maria The summer is over, Misail Alexandr. You and I shall try to balance our accounts. We have done a lot of work, a lot of thinking, and we are the better for it – all honour and glory to us – we have succeeded in self-improvement; but have we had the slightest influence on the life around us, have we brought any benefit to anyone else whatever? No. Ignorance, uncleanness, drunkenness, an appallingly high infant mortality rate, everything remains as it was, before we came here, and no one is better for your having ploughed and sown, and my having wasted money and read books. Obviously we have been working only for ourselves.

Misail We have been sincere from beginning to end, and if anyone is sincere he can't be wrong.

Maria We were right but we haven't succeeded in accomplishing what we were right in. To begin with, our methods – aren't they mistaken? You want to be of use to the peasants, but the very fact of our buying an estate from the very start cut you off from any possibility of doing anything for them. Then if you work, dress, eat like a peasant you sanctify, by your authority, their heavy, clumsy dress, their horrible huts, their stupid beards, their poverty. If you worked for years and years for your whole life, what could you do against such elemental forces as wholesale ignorance, hunger, cold? Nothing. If one really wants to be of use, one must get out of the narrow circle of social work, and try to act more fundamentally.

Misail How? How?

Maria Another medium is needed. What is wanted is a loud energetic propaganda. Why is it that music, for example, is so alive, so popular, so powerful? Because the musician or singer communicates with thousands at once. Precious, precious art! Art gives us wings and carries us far, far away. Anyone who is sick of filth, of petty, mercenary interest, anyone who is reviled, wounded and indignant, can find peace and satisfaction only in the beautiful.

Noise off.

What's that?

Misail A door banging. (*Pause.*) There are some pictures for you. From Paris.

Maria No. Listen.

Misail It's Ivan. He's got a gun. Moisey is running away from him. He's shouting. He's mad. What should I do?

Maria I don't know. We are living among animals. Let them bite out each other's throats.

Misail He's sitting on the ground. He's crying.

Maria Where is Papa?

Misail He's crying.

Maria Oh God, how much longer must we live among those animals? Go and wash, Misail. You've been in the fields.

Misail I know I've been in the fields . . . I've been in the fields. I'll wash.

Ivan calls off, 'Misail. Misail.' He enters.

Ivan Oh Misail. Misail. I wanted to kill him.

Misail There. Come on. Sit down. Come, come. Here we are. There.

Maria is looking at a picture. He goes over to her.

That's nice. Yes, it would suit you. Beautiful. Beautifully. Maria. Maria. (*She's crying.*)

Maria It's a pity you didn't mend that door. The rest of the house is so cold. There's a draught. It's terrible to live in the country. Terrible. Oh dear, if only Father's visit were over.

Prokofy has given Misail Alexandr a letter.

Prokofy An orderly came with it, Misail Alexandr.

Misail I am to go to see the Governor.

Prokofy It can't be for anything good. I suppose they will punish you.

Misail An interview at nine in the morning.

Prokofy You see. There are business rules for everyone. Rules for governors. Rules for priests. Rules for generals. Rules for doctors. Every class has its rules and regulations. But you haven't kept at your rules. And you can't be allowed. Ah well. I'll have to manage by myself then.

Misail No. I can still help. I'll never get work in this weather.

Prokofy It beats me. You looking for work. With your in-laws. What about your old friend?

Misail Andrey Ivanov? He's laid up.

Prokofy Well, if you keep your nose clean you're all right with us. If not . . . we have to watch it, we do.

Misail Where are we going?

Prokofy To the slaughter yards. I have some business there. Gech!

They set off. Wind. It's dark. There are carcasses hanging up in the slaughter yard. Figures in the background.

Prokofy Simeon. Hey. Simeon. Where are you? I've got something for you. Who's that over there? Nikolka?

Misail The stench.

Prokofy It's a slaughterhouse. It wouldn't smell like the spring. This cold. Misail Alexandr, be good to yourself. Warm up. You don't drink. Your wife ran off and you don't drink. (*He drinks from a flask.*)

Misail She hasn't run off.

Prokofy She's gone home to Father and you've come to us. I don't know about anything else. If there's anything better in this whole world than a little bit of bread dipped in kvass in the warm it's a nice drop of vodka out in the cold.

Misail Why are we here as early as this? Prokofy? You don't deal wholesale. You're a butcher.

Prokofy A butcher. (*Chop of his hand.*) Gech! But when there's a meat shortage, each man must turn his hand where he can. Me, I'm doing a bit of selling wholesale on the quiet.

Misail What are you selling? Why haven't we brought it with us?

Prokofy Misail Alexandr. In business don't ask the awkward questions. Learn first what questions to ask. Price. Payment. Quality. That kind of thing. But if you want to know, I haven't brought it till I'm sure of the market. I've left the beast where I found it. Frozen.

Misail What is it?

Prokofy A horse.

Misail What?

Prokofy You know him. He used to pull a cab.

Misail But you can't sell people a horse.

Prokofy Not me. I'm a good butcher. I don't sell people horse flesh. It'd be more than I'm worth. Simeon can use it.

He's a dealer. Where is he? He must be in the shed. You stay here and keep that shut. Do you hear me? I hope I don't have to impress on you the need for discretion.

He exits.

Misail Pools of blood. Snow. It's cold. O God. O Holy Mother. Help us sinners.

Wind.

SCENE ELEVEN

At Mme Azhogina's. Preparation for the evening's rehearsal. Refreshments. Among those present are Mme Azhogina, her daughters, Andrey Ivanov, Mme Mufke, Anyuta Blagovo, Cleopatra.

Mme Azhogina Now my dear, this is your first rehearsal but you musn't be nervous.

Cleopatra Oh, but I am. I know I shall make a fool of myself.

Mme Azhogina Nonsense.

Anyuta You'll be all right, Cleo. Come and get some tea.

Mme Azhogina That's right, my dear. I was just talking to Madame Mufke about superstition before you came in. My goodness, my whole life has been waging war against superstition. I always try and arrange anything important for the thirteenth of the month and I always have three candles on the table to encourage the servants.

Anyuta If you feel like that you shouldn't stay . . . If you don't care to take part, let's go. I don't mind.

Cleopatra No, I must stay.

Mme Azhogina Have you met Madame Mufke? Mademoiselle Poloznev?

Cleopatra Who is she?

Anyuta Madame Mufke.

Cleopatra I know, but who is she?

Anyuta I don't know.

Cleopatra Where does everyone go while we rehearse?

Anyuta Oh, they stay and watch.

Cleopatra Is that where we play?

Anyuta Yes. They've put out the chairs. You see?

A Guest Doesn't she look odd? What is she wearing?

Mme Mufke Such a mouse too.

Guest Look at her now. Cleopatra, Queen of the Nile.

Cleopatra (*looking at her script*) I can't read properly, there's something wrong with my eyes.

Anyuta Cleo!

Mme Azhogina Now. Everybody. I think you ought to take your places and we should begin. We're late already. Now. It is the beginning of the third act. Will you turn to the right page? Are we ready Mr Stage Manager? Good. Now you know what this represents. This is the road. This is the inn. Madame Mufke? Thank you, Madame. Thank you. Monsieur Berlichev? Where is Monsieur Berlichev?

Lisa I don't know, Mama.

Guest He's in the billiard room.

Mme Azhogina Well, go and get him then. We will wait. I am so sorry, my dears.

Cleopatra I am on at the beginning.

Anyuta Well, get ready then.

Cleopatra Oh, Anyuta.

Anyuta You are a goose.

Cleopatra I feel a little unwell.

Misail Alexandr enters.

Mme Azhogina Misail Alexandr. How good to see you. Will you have some tea?

Misail No, thank you. Is my wife here? I was looking for her.

Mme Azhogina She hasn't been with us all the week. We were speaking of her earlier on. We do miss her.

Berlichev enters.

Berlichev My dear lady, forgive me.

Mme Azhogina It is not good. A real artist is not late for his rehearsal, Monsieur Berlichev. Have you got your script? Get Monsieur Berlichev his script, Lisa. Where is it?

Berlichev I think I must have left it in the billiard room.

Mme Azhogina Well, really.

Berlichev I'm so sorry.

Mme Azhogina Indeed.

Misail Good evening, Anyuta (*She bows.*) I've come back to town. Cleo, why are you looking so worried? Why are you clutching the script like that?

Cleopatra I'm so excited. I'm so frightened. Misail, what shall I do?

Misail About what?

Cleopatra I am in the play.

Misail You?

Cleopatra Yes. I have been coming here with Anyuta for weeks. Papa doesn't know. I don't care. I tell him nothing now. If one has to lie to him that is *his* fault, is it not? Why are you here?

Misail I'm looking for Maria.

Cleopatra She isn't here.

Misail I know. I can see.

Cleopatra But why are you back in town? Father is very hurt that you have written nothing to him. You ought to have asked his blessing on the marriage. But really he is very much pleased. He says that it will raise you in the eyes of society, and that under the influence of Maria Victorovna you will begin to take a more serious view of life. We talk of nothing but you in the evening now, and yesterday he actually said 'Our Misail'. I'm glad. It seems as though he had some plan in his mind. I fancy he wants to set you an example and be the first to speak.

Misail What are you wearing, Cleo?

Cleopatra Is there something wrong with it?

Misail No. No. It's just that it's unlike you, that's all.

Cleopatra Is it all right? I read a great deal now. Thanks to your wife and to Boris. They have been my salvation. They have made me feel alive. In the old days I used to lie awake at night and think about what a lot of sugar we were using or if the cucumbers were too salty. Nowadays I still lie awake at night but I have different thoughts. Half my life has been passed in such a foolish and cowardly way. I despise my past. I am ashamed of it. And I think of Papa as my enemy. But how grateful I am to Maria and

Boris. He is such a wonderful person. They have opened my eyes. (*She coughs.*) What weakness. Boris says all city-bred girls are anaemic. From doing nothing. And he's right, of course. Absolutely right. We ought to work.

Mme Azhogina Mademoiselle Poloznev. Where is she?

Lisa We are waiting for you.

Cleopatra Oh. Oh dear, yes.

Mme Azhogina Now. The Countess and her companion. Yes, I think here, as indicated. The carriage is broken, the Countess sends Varvara into the inn.

They start, Cleopatra faltering.

Mme Mufke 'Child, give me my shawl.' (*To Mme Azhogina.*) Shouldn't she curtsy?

Mme Azhogina Perhaps.

Mme Mufke You should curtsy. (*She curtsies.*) *After* you give me the shawl.

Mme Azhogina Your line, Cleopatra.

Cleopatra 'Is it correct do you suppose for me to enter into such a place?'

Mme Mufke 'Is it correct?'

Cleopatra doesn't speak.

Mme Azhogina What is the line?

Mme Mufke Really.

Cleopatra I . . .

Lisa Page four. The top.

Mme Mufke 'Is it correct?'

Cleopatra faints.

Mme Azhogina Oh dear, oh dear, the poor child.

Misail and Anyuta pull her out of the crowd, Andrey carrying her.

Misail Cleo, Cleo. What is it? Cleo.

Guest A drink. A drink. Some tea.

Anyuta I knew we shouldn't have come. I knew it.

Andrey Let's take her out.

Misail Yes.

Mme Azhogina Yes, that is the thing to do.

They exit.

Get her home as soon as you can. She should rest.

She holds Misail back.

Misail Alexandr, forgive me, but naturally I know about these things. Your sister is pregnant. I am quite sure of it. I have thought so all along. I am quite convinced of it. Please ask her not to come here again.

SCENE TWELVE

Misail Alexandr and the Governor.

Governor M. Poloznev. I have asked you to call on me because it has come to our notice that you are likely to repeat your mistakes of a year ago.

I have before me a letter dated then in which your father asks the Marshal of the Nobility to bring to your notice the incompatibility of the life you had chosen with the rank to which you were born. Your recent marriage which enabled you to lead a life in the country full of sense and charity precluded any necessity for action on our part at the time. It seems now that official intervention in earnest is essential. I trust you will appreciate the delicacy with which the persons involved, particularly our honoured Alexandr Pavlovich, have brought this matter to my notice. His Excellency the Marshal spoke to me personally at a reception last evening. However, even now I shall not pursue the matter officially. But you must understand that your conduct does not go unnoticed and I suggest to you these alternatives: either you give up this life which you should have long since outgrown, or you move to a town where you are not so well known. You must realise that your conduct implicates all of us. Not only your family but all of us. Are you a vegetarian?

Misail No, Your Excellency. I eat meat.

SCENE THIRTEEN

Andrey Ivanov's lodgings. Cleopatra is pregnant. Andrey Ivanov is in bed. Cleopatra has finished reading to him.

Cleopatra There. Enough. (*She coughs.*)

Andrey That's lies for you. That's what lying does for you. The soul of the righteous man is smooth as a pebble. But the soul of the sinful man is like unto pumice stone. The soul of the righteous man is clear like oil, but the soul of the sinful man is like tar. We must labour; we must mourn; we must fall sick. He who labours not and mourns not neither shall he inherit the kingdom of heaven.

Cleopatra Where's my darning?

Andrey Woe. Woe unto them that are well fed, woe unto the mighty, woe unto the rich, woe unto the usurer, for the kingdom of heaven is not his. Grass doth wither. Iron doth rust.

TICKET
TOCYN

Sherman Cymru
Senghennydd Road/
Ffordd Senghennydd
Cardiff/Caerdydd
CF24 4YE

Ticket Office/Swyddfa Docynnau

029 2064 6900
tickets@shermancymru.co.uk
shermancymru.co.uk

National Theatre Wales

A PROVINCIAL LIFE

Tue 13 Mar 2012 at 7:30PM

THEATRE/THEATR 1, Door/Drws B

Row/Rhes D, Seat/Seddi 21

£15.00

Here are your tickets for Sherman Cymru – we hope you enjoy your visit. Please check your tickets carefully to make sure that everything is correct. If you find that you can't make it to this event, check **shermancymru.co.uk/booking** for information about what to do. Please make sure that you arrive in good time – for some shows we can't allow anyone into the theatre after the show has started. Finally, please don't use cameras or recording equipment in the theatres and do make sure that your mobile phones, pagers and digital alarms are turned off.

Dyma'ch tocynnau ar gyfer Sherman Cymru – gobeithiwn y byddwch chi'n mwynhau eich ymweliad. Byddwch mor garedig ag edrych yn ofalus ar eich tocynnau i wneud yn siŵr fod popeth yn gywir. Os na allwch ddod i'r digwyddiad hwn wedi'r cwbl, yna gallwch gael gwybodaeth am beth i'w wneud ar **shermancymru.co.uk/archebu**. Sicrhewch eich bod yn cyrraedd mewn da bryd – ni fydd yn bosib i ni ganiatau mynediad i'r theatr i rai perfformiadau unwaith bydd y sioe honno wedi dechrau. Yn olaf, byddwch mor garedig â pheidio â defnyddio camerâu nag offer recordio yn y theatrau, a sicrhewch fod eich ffonau symudol, eich peiriannau galw a'ch larymau digidol wedi eu diffodd.

A Registered Charity/Elusen Gofrestredig
Company Number/Rhif y Cwmni 06002090

Cleopatra And lies do rot the soul. I must finish this.
Here, shall I mark the place? There. At home our cook
used to do all the darning. But I don't mind. You must
rest, Andrey Ivanov. The doctor is coming this evening.
I hope he won't be late. Misail hasn't seen him yet. Are
you all right? You shall have some bread later with your
tea. The orderly came again today and I know where he
comes from and who sends these gifts. Anyuta Blagovo.
I recognise her scent. Tell me what is it that stops people
from acting as they really desire. What is the compulsion?
Anyuta loves Misail. She loves me like a sister and she
knows I'm doing the right thing and envies me I think, in
her heart of hearts. But she will not visit us. She shuns us
and she's scared. If only you knew how she loves Misail
Alexandr. I'm the only person she has ever told about it.
She used to take me into the darkest part of their garden
and whisper it to me. She'll never marry because she
loves him. She always sends him things. She's a funny
girl. Why make such a secret of it? I was funny like that
myself once. But now I've left that house I'm afraid of no
one. Living at home I had no idea what happiness was,
but now I wouldn't change places with the Queen. Are
you asleep, Andrey? (*Pause.*) I wish Boris would come.

Misail Alexandr comes in.

Cleopatra You're early.

Misail We finished the job.

Cleopatra What will you do tomorrow?

Misail I don't know yet.

Cleopatra I've got your dinner warm.

Misail I'll wash.

Cleopatra No. sit down. You look tired. I've got
something to tell you. Here you are. What's that?

Misail A letter. I collected it at the post office.

Cleopatra Who's it from?

Misail Maria.

Cleopatra Open it.

He doesn't.

Misail.

Misail Yes? What were you going to tell me?

Pause. She sews. He eats. Andrey sleeps.

Cleopatra Boris is back. He's coming here this evening.

Misail I thought you looked pale. That accounts for it. Are you glad he's back?

Cleopatra Oh, Misail. I'm so happy.

They embrace.

You work so hard.

Misail You must take care of yourself. You're not sleeping. I know. I hear you.

Cleopatra Do you think I am ill? Not at all. Boris sounded me and he said I was perfectly well. But health is not what matters. It is not so important. Tell me. Am I not right? Oh, Misail. When the baby is here I will do everything. The cleaning. The washing. Everything. I will be truly independent. I will become a teacher. I'm not so stupid. Or a doctor's assistant.

Misail Who'll look after the baby then?

Cleopatra I will. I will look after him as well.

Misail Him?

Cleopatra Yes. It will be a boy. I know it. I should think he will be like you. Also Boris.

They embrace. Andrey Ivanov stirs.

Misail (*going to him*) Are you feeling better today?

Cleopatra He's much better. I've been reading to him. I think he might get up tomorrow and sit in a chair.

Andrey With God all things are possible.

Cleopatra We'll have finished this book, Misail, soon.

Misail I'll go to the library and borrow another.

Misail goes back to the table and eats. The front doorbell goes.

Cleopatra That will be Boris. Hand me my shawl. He'll scold if I go to the door without it.

She goes out. Misail opens his letter. Andrey watches him. He puts it back in the envelope.
Cleopatra re-enters with the Doctor.

Cleopatra Misail. Misail. Look who's here. (*She coughs.*)

Doctor There. There.

Cleopatra But look, Misail. How splendid. Look at his tiepin. And his handkerchief. (*She pulls it out. It is red.*) How beautiful.

Doctor You can have it.

Misail And a new suit.

Doctor No.

Misail How many?

Cleopatra laughs.

Cleopatra Misail and I have a game. We try to count your suits.

Misail Nine.

Cleopatra Eight. (*She coughs.*)

Doctor Neither. Sit down. You mustn't talk so much. Now. You chatter like a magpie.

Misail You've left the army.

Doctor I have. I finished my work. I'm going to Europe to study. I'm going to look into inoculations against typhus and cholera. I want to teach in the university if I can get a post. The army doesn't suit me. I want to study as much now as I ever did.

Cleopatra Will you have some tea?

Doctor If you please. Last time I was at home you were still living at your old nurse's house. What happened?

Misail Her son Prokofy told us to go. I don't blame him. We weren't respectable. Andrey took us in.

Doctor And your friend in the country?

Misail Ivan Cheprakov? His mother bought the estate back off Dolzhikov after we left at a knock-down price. The villainous Moisey is going from strength to strength by report. Ivan came to live in town at one point. Hanging about and getting drunk. I gave him a job and he was quite good at it as it happens. And he became a regular workman. Working hard and stealing the oil and asking for tips and getting drunk when he got his wages. But then got bored with it and went back to the country where things are much as they were, I think.

Doctor And how are you, old man? Did you take what I sent you? Did he have some of it? You didn't.

Andrey Your honour.

Doctor What is it?

Andrey Permit me to tell you the truth, sir. We all walk in fear of the Lord. We all have to die. But someone really ought to tell you the truth and that is that the kingdom of heaven will not be yours.

Doctor Then there's nothing to be done about it, is there? There has to be someone in the other place. (*Pause.*) Now Cleopatra, you're tired.

Cleopatra coughs.

Listen to that. It's time to take your drops. Get them now. Then let us go into the next room so that I can sound you. And then you must rest. Look at you.

Cleopatra No. Oh, no.

Doctor Yes, I'm afraid so. Open your mouth. There, some tea. Better? Come along.

Cleopatra Bring your glass.

They go out. Cleo can be heard coughing. Misail takes out the letter.

Andrey What's that, our angel?

Misail A letter from my wife.

Andrey Oh.

Misail Listen to what she says. (*He reads.*) 'Dear good Misail Alexandr, our angel, as the old workman calls you. Farewell. I am going with my father to America for the exhibition. In a few days I shall be so far away from Dubetchnya it's impossible to think. It is as far and unfathomable as the sky and I long to be there in freedom. I am triumphant. I am mad. And you see how incoherent this letter is. Dear good one, forgive me. Give me my freedom, break the cord which still holds us together. My meeting and knowing you was a ray from heaven that lighted up my existence but our marriage was a mistake and I am oppressed now by the consciousness of it and I beseech you on my knees, my generous friend, quickly,

quickly before I start for the ocean, telegraph that you'll agree to correct our mistake and remove this stone from my wings and my father who will undertake all arrangements promises not to burden you too much with formalities. And so I am free to fly whither I will. Yes. Be happy and God bless you. Forgive me, a sinner. I am well. I am wasting money, doing all sorts of silly things. And I thank God every minute that such a bad woman as I has no children. I sing and have success, but it's truly not an infatuation. No, it's my haven. My cell. To which I go for peace. King David had a ring and on it was inscribed "Everything passes". When one is sad these words make one happy and when one is happy they make one sad. I have got myself a ring like that with Hebrew letters on it and this talisman keeps me from infatuations. All things will pass. Life will pass. One wants nothing. Or at least one wants nothing but the sense of freedom, for when anyone is free he wants nothing, nothing, nothing. Break the thread. A warm hug to you and your sister. Forgive me and forget. Your.'

Pause.

Andrey Can I have some bread? She offered me some.

Misail Yes. Yes. She has her ring with an inscription on it. He has his work and a professor's chair to look forward to. Only my sister and myself are left with the old things.

The Doctor comes back in.

Doctor She's resting. Is there more tea?

Misail How do you think she is?

Doctor (*cries*) My dear friend.

Misail What is it?

Doctor She is so good. It's sad. It's so sad. But it's hopeless, my dear. It's hopeless. You hate me. Both of you. And you think I have behaved badly. And you are right. but how can I regret what has happened? One must love. We ought to love, oughtn't we? There would be no life without love. You're not free if you cannot love. Anyone who fears and avoids love is not free. Is he?

SCENE FOURTEEN

The Poloznev house. Misail and his Father.

Father What have you come here for?

Misail I don't know. My sister is very ill. She can't live long.

Father It is two years since you were last here. You didn't listen to me then. You went your own way. Now obviously you must pay for it. As you sow so shall you reap.

Misail You ought to take care. Frivolity doesn't become you. You haven't long left.

Father What do you want?

Misail I don't know. I love you. I am unutterably sorry that we are apart. I love you. I have always loved you. But I was luckier than her. She doesn't forget. She won't forgive you, Father. Talk of you makes her worse.

Father And who is to blame for that?

Misail I suppose it is my fault. I have been to blame in many things. But tell me what kind of life did you give us? How is it that in not one of your houses did I meet one person who could teach me how to live? Your houses are nests of vice where lives are made away and men stupefy themselves with cards and vodka and scandal and hypocrisy and cant so as not to notice the abortive melodramas that go on in the drawing rooms.

Father We looked after you. We brought you up. We cared for you in your childhood.

Misail My childhood. I had no childhood. We had no childhood. I should kill you. All I can remember of my childhood is tortured dogs driven mad for amusement with tin cans tied to their tails. Or live sparrows plucked naked by boys and flung into the river for fun. A long, long, long series of obscure lingering miseries which I have looked on continually in this town. I cannot understand what this thirty thousand people lives for. What they read the Gospel for, why they pray, why they read books and magazines. What has been gained from all that has been said and written in the past if we are still possessed by the same darkness and hatred of three hundred years ago? What would it matter if the earth opened up tomorrow and swallowed us up? Who would know that we had even been here at all?

Father You speak to me like this in my own house. Go away. Get out. What are you? Who are you?

Misail It is I, Misail Alexandr. What does that mean? Oh, my sister. My mother.

Father Well, you'll get nothing from me. Tell her. Both of you, either of you. If you suffer for what you have done I don't pity you. Tell her that. What I have done I will bear it. What I have done I will bear it.

Misail waves his hand and goes away. Wind. Figures in the dark.

Misail Alexandr, alone.

Misail My wife had a ring and on it was inscribed,
'Everything passes'. If I needed an inscription for a ring
I would write: 'Nothing passes', for I believe nothing can
pass without leaving a trace and that everything we do,
however small, has significance in our present and in our
future. What I have done has made some difference. For
example, people don't laugh at me now. When I walk
past shops they don't throw water over me. They have
got used to me. And they don't think it strange to see
me walking through the streets carrying a bucket of paint
or climbing a ladder to mend a roof, even though I do
belong to a family and ought to know better. I have
worked hard and am considered a first-class workman;
people give me contracts now and are glad to. Andrey
Ivanov can't organise the men as he used to and most of
that kind of work has fallen to me. I think I am a good
foreman. I run about the town looking for jobs for us.
I engage the men and I pay them. Most of the time I pay
them with money I have to borrow, then I have to borrow
more to pay off the interest. But people are civil to me. In
some of the houses where we work they give me tea and
the children and young girls come and look at me in their
curious and compassionate way. I have grown older and
have become silent, almost stern. I rarely laugh and am
told that I have grown to be like Andrey Ivanov and that
like him I bore the men with my high moral tone. My
father has aged greatly. In the evening he walks up and
down near his house. I never go to see him. On working
days I am busy from morning till night and on holidays,
if the weather is fine, I take my little niece (my sister
reckoned on a boy but the child is a girl) and I walk in
the cemetery with her. There I stand or sit near the grave

that is so dear to me and tell the child that that is where her mother lies. Sometimes by the graveside I meet Anyuta Blagovo. We stand in silence or talk of Cleopatra or the child or how sad life is in this world. And when we leave the cemetery we walk in silence and she slows down her pace on purpose so that we can walk together. The little girl pulls at her hand very happily. And we stop at the gates with the child still between us. Then Anyuta says goodbye to me and goes on alone and no one that met her could imagine, looking at her, that she had just been talking with me or even nursing the child.